D0833143

POMPEII AND ITS MUSEUMS

POMPEII AND ITS MUSEUMS

Newsweek / GREAT MUSEUMS OF THE WORLD

NEW YORK, N.Y.

**GREAT MUSEUMS
OF THE WORLD**

Editorial Director—Henry A. La Farge

POMPEII AND ITS MUSEUMS

Introduction by:
Michael Grant

Texts by:
Antonio de Simone
Gemma Verchi

Design:
Fiorenzo Giorgi

Published by:
NEWSWEEK, INC.
& ARNOLDO MONDADORI EDITORE

This volume is being published simultaneously under the
title of *The Art and Life of Pompeii and Herculaneum*

2nd Printing October 1979

ISBN: Clothbound Edition 0-88225-243-7
ISBN: Deluxe Edition 0-88225-218-6

©1979—Arnoldo Mondadori Editore—CEAM—Milan

All rights reserved. Printed and bound in Italy
by Arnoldo Mondadori, Verona.

INTRODUCTION

By Michael Grant

In the eighteenth century, when Pompeii and Herculaneum were being rediscovered, it was declared that "the grand object of all travel is to see the shores of the Mediterranean." The sage, Dr. Samuel Johnson, who made this assertion, was accustomed to making pontifical statements, and some have thought that here he was going rather too far. Yet, despite pollution, despite politics, many stretches of these shorelands still retain an unequaled beauty. And perhaps the most beautiful region of all (and the most fertile as well) is Campania is southwestern Italy. The coastline of this land, which begins some ninety miles southeast of Rome, includes the incomparable Bay of Naples. Above the bay rises Mount Vesuvius, which is more formidable than its height of under 4,200 feet suggests. West of Vesuvius is Naples itself, while the remains of Herculaneum stand to the southwest of the mountain, and Pompeii to its southeast. Naples was already a great town in ancient times—but Pompeii and Herculaneum were relatively small, numbering some 25,000 and 5,000 inhabitants respectively.

Naples was founded by the Greeks (ca. 650 B.C.), who called it Neapolis, the New City; they colonized this entire coastal area, and settled at both Pompeii and Herculaneum, or had trading posts there. Subsequently these two smaller towns (though never Naples itself), fell under the temporary influence of one or more of the powerful Etruscan city-states which lay northwest of the still relatively minor power of Rome. In the fifth century B.C., the dominant role in the area fell to the Samnites, tough Italian hillsmen who came from fortified strongpoints in the center of the peninsula. But Rome, now rising rapidly, defeated the Samnites, and annexed Campania—which became their first window upon the Mediterranean. In this process, they took over Pompeii and Herculaneum (310-302 B.C.), though as was their wise practice, these towns were no doubt left to govern themselves. Nevertheless, in 91 B.C., both Pompeii and Herculaneum joined a violent Italian rebellion against Roman domination. But they were apparently reduced by the Roman general Sulla, who, when he later became dictator, made Pompeii a "colony," injecting a draft of Roman settlers but leaving the place's autonomy intact under a new system of government.

After that, Pompeii enjoyed another century and a half of peaceful existence and prosperous growth. A harbor town alongside the small river Sarnus (Sarno), serving a rich inland zone, it was also a small but bustling center of wine and oil production (although Pompeian wine was said to give one a hangover); its local industries included wool and woolen goods, and it exported a famous fish-sauce (see note at end), fruit, volcanic stone (tufa) and millstones.

For a long time Vesuvius had remained quiet. Indeed, it had never erupted since the beginning of recorded history, though Strabo, a Greek geographer at the turn of our era, rightly deduced from its appearance that the crater had once been volcanic. A warning was given (though not heeded) in the reign of Nero, during the month of February A.D. 62, when a severe earthquake badly damaged the towns around the mountain, Pompeii worse than any of them. The damage was so severe that, when the fatal eruption took place seventeen years later, only a very few of the town's public and private buildings had by then been fully restored.

The eruption took place in A.D. 79—soon after the accession of the emperor Titus—so that we are now celebrating its nineteen hundredth anniversary. August 24, A.D. 79, dawned clear and hot. There had been earth tremors for several days, and springs had dried up, but probably no one was particularly worried. Then came the sudden, appalling explosion. We can tell more or less what took place from analyses of the deposits which buried the whole region, and from a famous account by Pliny the younger, the literary nephew of the famous encyclopaedist and historian of the same name. The latter personage, the elder Pliny, happened at the time to be the commander of the Roman fleet at Misenum (Miseno), nineteen miles away at the northwestern end of the Bay of Naples. His nephew was with him, and in later years wrote his eyewitness recollections of the eruption in two letters to the historian Tacitus. A vast dark cloud had appeared across the bay, and had blotted out the sun. "Its general appearance can best be expressed as being like an [umbrella] pine rather than any other tree, for it rose to a great height on a sort of trunk and then split off into branches, I imagine because it was thrust upwards by the first blast and then left unsupported as the pressure subsided, or else it was borne down by its own weight so that it spread out and gradually dispersed. Sometimes it looked white, sometimes blotched and dirty, according to the amount of soil and ashes it carried with it."

The elder Pliny, receiving a desperate message from a woman friend along the coast, ordered the warships out (his nephew is careful to point out that it was not for her sake alone), and made for a point near Herculaneum, west of the volcano. But bad conditions and falls of debris made it impossible for him to land, and he sailed on instead to Stabiae (Castellamare di Stabia, south of Vesuvius), where he spent the night at a friend's villa near the sea. On the following morning, however, Pliny, who was a fat man, was overcome by fumes on the beach, and fell down and died. It was not until two days of pitch darkness, only broken terrifyingly by lightning and the flames of electric storms, that his body could be recovered.

By that time, Pompeii had long since been obliterated. Indeed, since the eruption started in the late morning of the 24th, more than a man's height of ash must already have fallen over the city by what would ordinarily have been sunset on the same day. The surface of solid basalt, which had plugged the cone of the volcano since before the beginning of history, was suddenly shattered by an overwhelming build-up of heat and pressure from far beneath the earth. A vast mass of lava and boulders leapt thousands of feet into the air, and crashed down like a rain of bombs, followed by an impenetrable cloud of incandescent pumice—white, grey and greyish in color—which covered the ground of Pompeii up to a height of six or eight feet. Then, in the night that followed, the sides of the old volcanic cone collapsed inward, causing a fresh series of explosive shocks which convulsed the whole region with violent earthquakes. A torrent of steam, ash, cinders and dust rose precipitously into the sky and hurtled downward again in a thick, seething mass, which blanketed the ground with an additional seven feet of deposit. It was not until late in the day of the 26th that a dim light finally reappeared to reveal a scene of unprecedented desolation.

A different fate had befallen Herculaneum, which had been overwhelmed not by pumice and ashes but by a torrid, treacly sea of mud. At least, however, the slow approach of this wave had enabled most of the population to get away in time. At Pompeii, many more people were taken by surprise, and the number of fatalities amounted to at least two thousand. The first victims were struck down by lava, rocks and falling masonry, and then many more were suffocated by ash, and, above all, asphyxiated by the sulphurous fumes and lethal chloride-impregnated gases that the belching crater emitted. Innumerable dramatic signs of these tragic casualties were still to be seen when the excavators came upon the site. A room in a house, where a group had taken refuge, was found closed with an iron shutter: the remains of twelve people were discovered inside. On the threshold of another house, its mistress and three of her maids lay dead, her jewelry and money scattered around. In one building, the top story crumbled and fell in ruins, killing seven children inside. The priests of the shrine of the Egyptian goddess Isis set out to seek safety, carrying with them the treasures of the temple. But one by one, at different points, they collapsed, scattering their valuables around them; the last of them to remain alive and on their feet took refuge inside a house, where one of them broke through two walls with an axe, but to no avail because he and his companions all perished.

The survival of small material objects was extraordinary and uncanny. Eggs and fish were still to be seen where there had not been time to eat them. At an eating-house, eighty-one loaves remained, carbonized, in the oven, where they had been placed only a few seconds before the building was overwhelmed. At another inn, gladiators did not have time to finish their drinks and left their trumpets behind as they fled. In their own barracks, sixty gladiators succumbed, including several in chains, as well as a richly jeweled woman who was paying one of the inmates a visit. Not many beasts of burden lost their lives in the city, because escapers had mobilized the rest to take them away. But dead dogs have been found, and one of them offers a horrible testimony, because it gnawed the adjoining dead body of its master before it, too succumbed. Outside the walls the casualties continued. In one of the extensive cemeteries in the city outskirts, thirty-four men, women and children hid themselves away in a tomb, taking with them large food supplies including a goat, but there, goat and all, they met their deaths. Efforts to get away by sea proved equally unsuccessful since, even when people managed to struggle through to the coast, scorching waves and wind made embarkation impossible.

In the very first days after the eruption, before the jumble of debris had solidified, efforts were made to salvage the valuables that lay beneath it. Parties of survivors—rescuers or robbers, or both—saved what they could, using the tallest parts of the buried buildings which still rose above the devastation, to guide them. In particular, bronze statues and marble facings in the Forum were removed. The visitors to this dreadful buried world left graffiti: one, written by a Jew or a Christian, just simply says "Sodom and Gomorrah." The emperor Titus attempted relief measures, but nothing much seems to have come of them.

During the long centuries that followed, fresh townships were gradually established near the former city of Pompeii, and the other obliterated places roundabout. But from the ancient sites there was total silence, until the eighteenth century when gradual, tentative, unsystematic discoveries began to reveal the unimaginable riches that lay far beneath the surface. The impact of these finds on the beginnings of modern Italian archaeology, on the thoughts of German writers such as Goethe, and on the interior decorators of Western Europe (where, by coincidence, artistic taste was turning toward Neo-Classicism and ready for such influences) makes a whole series of fascinating stories.

The activities of Sir William Hamilton, British envoy to the King of Naples from 1764 to 1800, are also well worth notice. Many valuable objects from Pompeii and Herculaneum found their way into his own private collection. However, he was subsequently obliged to sell a considerable number of them "because he had spent so much on Emma," his beautiful young wife, who later became the mistress of Admiral Horatio Nelson (and put on a lot of weight). Then Sir William formed a second collection, which was sunk on *H.M.S. Colossus* off the Scilly Islands in 1798. The ship has now been salvaged and the fragmentary remains of his treasures acquired in 1975 by the British Museum are now being meticulously reassembled so that they can be placed on exhibition.

A special tribute must be made to Giuseppe Fiorelli, with whose appointment to look after these sites (1860–75) systematic excavation began. It was he who first adopted the practice of restoring the old buildings in order to make them comprehensible to visitors: so that the ruined cities constitute entire museums in themselves, and museums of the most spectacular possible kind—amply justifying, it will surely be agreed, the inclusion of the present volume in the series entitled "Museums of the World." Fiorelli's desire was to preserve as many as possible of the objects that were found on the spot, instead of taking away the most spectacular items and not caring what happened to the rest of the site (though, in today's conditions, it has proved more prudent to remove important objects to the Naples Museum). Moreover, Fiorelli invented an ingenious way of recapturing the living appearance of the people whose remains have been found at Pompeii. He noted that in many cases the ash deposit had solidified so closely around the dead bodies that, after decomposition, their forms were still exactly preserved around the empty space that had thus been created. By inserting a tube into this hollow space (after the bones had been removed), and then injecting a specially designed solution of liquid plaster, which subsequently hardened, the shape of the body was reproduced. The detailed results of this process are astonishing. Even the outlines of clothing and sandals, the traces of hair on head and face and body, are meticulously preserved; even the facial expressions of the death agony have come down to us over the centuries. Only last year, the Fiorelli technique was applied once again to two new discoveries, victims of the eruption who were suffocated in an out-of-town cemetery. One of the dead was a young girl who wore silver bracelets and had taken a bronze statuette with her when she unavailingly took refuge.

This is macabre. And yet it is also touching and *enjoyable*. Its enjoyableness raises interesting problems about what sort of persons we ourselves are, and how we feel. The Japanese writer, Haruko Ichikawa, was more worried about the posthumous fate of the people who were thus so surprisingly preserved. "It would not," he said, "be very pleasant to become part of a show excavated after two thousand years." But equally relevant is the question why we ourselves find so much pleasure in the show.

However, it is a question that has to be broadened, to include the impact upon us not only of the corpses but of the entire dead city of Pompeii as it is uniquely set out for our inspection—and entertainment. "Many a calamity," said Goethe, "has happened in the world, but never one that caused so much entertainment to posterity as this one." Such "enjoyment of ruins" seemed to the novelist Henry James a heartless, perverse pleasure, and it was the *deadness* of Pompeii that struck Sir Walter Scott; as he walked around the empty streets in his old age, he muttered repeatedly "The City of the Dead! The City of the Dead!" One reason for his depression was no doubt diagnosed by his later fellow-author Malcolm Lowry, who declared that "it is as if you could hear *your own* real life plunging to its doom." Certainly, "remember that you too are mortal" is one of the messages that visitors cannot fail to carry away from the ghost site of Pompeii. But that is not all, for the real point of the site is the overpowering way in which it shows not only death, but *life and death* together, in inextricably close association. Life is in death, and death is in life; the place emits an all-pervading aura of being and not being at one and the same time.

This dualism is of course seen with the most arresting immediacy in the plaster casts of the men, women, boys and girls who were struck down and transfixed in midstride. They were ordinary human beings, people who had no doubt lived ordinary lives, but by an exceptional blow of fate were subjected to an extraordinary catastrophic misfortune, which has made them our companions today. It is they, the microcosms of the human condition, representatives of all humanity, who make Pompeii unique. And their uniqueness is underlined by the little piquant, everyday things in their lives which have survived alongside them: the remains of food, the schoolboy's inkpot, the dice and knuckle-bones for gambling, the lamps and bottles and jugs, the tradesman's stamp and carpenter's plane and doctor's intimate instruments, the half-finished work lying on the jeweler's bench, the garden ornaments (not to everyone's taste, but better than modern plastic gnomes), and the marble slab advising us that the freedman Januarius recommends the salt and fresh water baths of Marcus Crassus Frugi.

And then there are all those innumerable messages painted or incised on Pompeian walls. The painted inscriptions include a revealing collection of local election notices and propaganda. In contrast to Rome, where the emperor's shadow leaned more heavily, rivalry for the annually contested chief municipal offices of Pompeii remained extremely acute. At the time of the eruption, the election campaign of 79 was just heating up, and has left its mark in the pronouncements of countless canvassers. Some of these, I suspect, are really intended to work *against* the candidate they appear to favor. A certain Vatia, for example, is ostensibly supported by everyone "who is fast asleep" and "is a late drinker"—and by the pickpockets of the town. Another candidate has a rather damping testimonial: "his grandmother did a lot of hard work for him at his last election." And yet another has an indefatigable supporter in his "little girl-friend," which may not have been the best possible recommendation.

But what perhaps makes a stronger historical impact than anything else is the mass of graffiti on the walls. Unfortunately, they will offer little visual impression to the tourist, because they are just scratchy incisions, hard to see, and in any case many have now been removed to the Naples Museum, while others have just crumbled away. But first they were carefully listed, and copied; and they still have an enormous amount to yield to future research. Indeed, I doubt if there is any other single source that can tell us more about how the people of any part of the Roman Empire thought and felt.

A huge range of human activities is represented by these graffiti—politics, literature, grass-roots religion, lavatory humor, and above all (as today) sex in alarmingly diversified abundance. Sex appears in many paintings too, notably in some of the (at least) seven brothels that this small town provided. Sex is pretty open at Pompeii, and representations of the male organ are particularly abundant. An interesting question arises. Was it like this all over the Roman empire, or was the Greek culture of this particular region especially uninhibited? Since other towns do not furnish the wealth of material evidence that we have from Pompeii, we cannot give a certain answer. But it can at least be said that Pompeii and its neighboring towns, because of their civilized backgrounds, probably present the subject with greater artistry than would have been found elsewhere.

For that is the keynote of the entire Pompeian scene, and an astringent reminder to those who believe we have improved in every way since those ancient times. That is to say, whether morals have got better or not (as is hard to tell), the general standard of aesthetic achievement in the cities of Vesuvius is a great deal higher than could be found in almost any townships of similar size in the world of today. And, by the same token, the cultural amenities Pompeii and Herculaneum offered were far more impressive than anything comparable modern towns could offer. What town of 25,000 inhabitants nowadays has two elegant stone theaters, one large and one small? And what twentieth-century town has no less than four sets of public baths—not to speak of those that still may await discovery—equipped with a wide, luxurious range of club facilities, and decorated with graceful stucco facings on their walls and vaults? Moreover, as many as ten temples have come to light at Pompeii, which must have presented a distinguished appearance when they were whole; and although their surviving remains are comparatively insubstantial, they constitute a treasure house of information about ancient religion.

As to the city's amphitheater, there is the usual contradictory judgment to offer. Like others of its kind, it served the appallingly brutal purpose of gladiatorial duels—and it is good to know that in A.D. 59, because of spectator riots, the emperor Nero closed the arena for a time. And yet, architecturally, the great external arches of this Pompeian amphitheater, and its spacious auditorium, present a fine appearance. Furthermore, it is noteworthy that here, in so small a town, we have the oldest known permanent edifice of the kind anywhere in the world dating back to 80 B.C. An impressive early date must also be attributed to Pompeii's Basilica, a term for those imposing public halls of the pagan Roman world that were the ancestors of law courts, Christian basilicas, Italian *gallerie* and stock exchanges all in one. The Basilica at Pompeii was built about 100 B.C., at a date earlier than any basilica in Rome itself that has come down to us. This is only one of innumerable ways in which Pompeii contributes vastly to our knowledge of architectural history.

The Pompeian Basilica faces the city's Forum, the type of open city square which ranks high among the great achievements of ancient Italy's architecture and town planning. Surrounded, like Greek marketplaces but more impressively, by colonnades on three sides—the fourth being reserved for the city's main temple of Jupiter—the whole composition of the Forum at Pompeii must have been delightful and stimulating: a not unworthy ancestor of the central open spaces that are the glories of later Italian cities, culminating in the Piazza San Marco at Venice. To see the Pompeii Forum empty, though, is unnatural, and to that extent today's tourists serve a purpose, because they fill the unnaturally silent vacuum. For in ancient times these *Fora*, as Lord Clark aptly puts it, were "the open squares of Latin civilization, with their resistant masonry echoing the shouts of uninhibited extroversion."

And yet it is not the public but the private buildings of Pompeii that are most informative of all about the lives of its inhabitants. One of the desirable outcomes of the most recent excavations and researches has been a much wider knowledge of the various kinds of dwellings of the underprivileged and the poor (including in the city's later years, a partitioning of the larger houses into much smaller apartments). I hope a full-scale study of this subject may before long be written, to the great advantage of our sociological knowledge of the Roman world (which has also benefited enormously from our discoveries of small shops and inns of the city, and from revelations of the remarkable social mobility the place displayed). But it is, obviously, the residences of those who were better off that have proved the more lasting; it is they that have captured the imagination of posterity. Indeed, these surviving houses of Pompeii have been described, with some justification, as the most wonderful of all the monuments that antiquity has left for our inspection anywhere in the world.

They look inward, mainly deriving their light not from external windows but from courtyards within. Any visitor on a burning Campanian summer day can admire the way in which these architects sought and realized an ideal of coolness and peace amid the hot clatterings of the outside world. The main courtyard of these houses was a rectangular "atrium" (probably borrowed from the Etruscans), usually with an opening in the middle of its roof, located above a catch basin for the collection of rain water. Around the atrium were various rooms, and behind them, if there was space enough, lay an enclosed garden court or peristyle; and the largest houses had an open garden and orchard as well.

These dwellings sometimes attained dimensions of up to 700 square yards. And yet to modern eyes some features of their design are curiously unimpressive. For example, the rooms (especially the dining rooms) are often poky and diminutive—and kitchen and toilet facilities tend to be more than sketchy. Heating (excellent in the public baths) was inadequate in private houses—for the Pompeian winter can be perishingly cold—and window panes (again in contrast to the baths) were very rare or nonexistent, so that wooden shutters had to serve instead; and the artificial lighting, by torches or tapers or tallow candles, must have been ineffectual and smelly.

On the other hand the gardens were charming; their contents have been cleverly reconstructed, again by Fiorelli's technique of pouring plaster into the vacuums left by the vanished roots. But what is most remarkable of all—and once more reminds us of the high standard of general taste—was the interior decoration of these houses. Its main principles were two: wall surfaces should be covered all over with paintings applied directly to the surfaces of the walls themselves, and floors should be similarly covered from end to end with mosaics. True, panel paintings for the walls were not unknown, and no doubt rugs were at least occasionally placed on the floors. But neither of these practices became at all common, since both seemed to ancient ideas to upset the architectural lines of the house (for the same reason, furniture was, by modern standards, sparse). So ancient Pompeii, for decade after decade, provides us with a whole succession of wall paintings and floor mosaics, and this enormously varied, chronologically recordable series is an astonishing contribution to our knowledge of the ancient world. Some of these masterpieces, not only providing copies of vanished Greek painting which are of great importance to the art historians, but also comprising works that are entirely original, are shown by reproductions in this book. The technique employed—painting on a carefully prepared surface of lime mortar topped with coats of marble dust to create a shiny, brilliant surface—was an exacting and difficult process requiring great skill.

The paintings have customarily been classified in four successive styles, though they overlap and, in the light of more recent study, the arrangement stands in need of an overhaul. But it has helped to establish the main lines of development. The earliest kind of wall painting found at Pompeii, from early in the first century B.C., is the so-called Incrustation style (from *crusta,* a slab of marble) because, like Greek work of the previous century and earlier, it simulates the color contrasts of marble, alabaster or porphyry facings used to cover walls. Then, later in the same century, came the Second, or Architectural style, in which vivid representations of buildings offer daring, three-dimensional vistas of streets, houses and colonnaded halls, apparently in imitation of stage settings for theatrical performances, and designed so as to create the illusion that the rooms are larger than they actually are. From then onward, too, paintings show charmingly skillful rural scenes and still-life representations strangely anticipating the Dutch masterpieces of a later millennium.

The Third style, which overlapped with the Second and continued until about A.D. 50, abandoned this illusionistic opening up of internal spaces, reducing the painted forms to tenuous, plant-like candelabra, vines and garlands in which the architectural character had become scarcely more than ornament against the overall ground color. The Fourth Style, which started before the Third was over and is held to have continued until the life of Pompeii came to an 'end, is a somewhat meaningless designation covering a considerable diversity of pictorial motifs; and by far the greater part of Pompeii's surviving paintings belong to this period. Architectural patterns—enlivened with little figures and fabulous beasts—have become even more delicately ornamental. Fashionable also were scenes in which mythological themes abound: in the best of such pictures, faces and emotions are vividly suggested by a few bold and impressionistic brush-strokes. These are sympathetic portraits of real persons—presumably the owners of the houses—which astutely catch the moods of their sitters. Romantic, idyllic pastoral countrysides are also to be found, including Egyptian river scenes and exotic menageries. The amount of skill displayed in all these different kinds of paintings varies considerably. For one thing, some house owners may not have been too particular, thinking of the pictures as symbols of social standing and financial investments rather than works of art. And, besides, artists of every quality had to be pressed into service after the earthquake of A.D. 62, which had left such a large number of houses in need of complete redecoration. All the same, the level of accomplishment displayed by many of the painters is remarkable. Their achievements remain highly distinctive; their reddish grounds—the famous Pompeian red—stay in the mind, and so does their characteristically light and airy brushwork.

Floor mosaics, too, made up of little colored cubes of colored stone and marble arranged in beds of cement, became a typical, successful, and wonderfully durable art in Pompeii. According to the late Sir Mortimer Wheeler, it was *the* Roman art. The Greeks, in their early experiments in the medium, had envisaged these mosaic designs as alternatives to rugs in the middle of the floor spaces, or to mats beside the door. In Italy, and very notably in the Vesuvian cities, not only did this tradition continue, but another practice also arose, according to which the whole floor came to be envisaged as a single space, to be covered all over by a carpet-like mosaic of unified design. So Pompeian mosaics come in all sizes; and they include a great range of different colorful themes, manners and methods.

The most famous of the large-scale mosaics shows an elaborate scene of the Battle of Issus (333 B.C.) between Alexander the Great and the Persians, adapted from a Greek picture that is now lost. There are also innumerable other fine examples, many now in the Naples Museum along with the paintings. Among them are charming miniature mosaics, made up of particularly tiny cubes arranged in sinuously curving designs; not all of these compositions were inset in floors, some of them being mounted on marble trays. One of these miniature pieces is a strikingly effective female portrait; others show theatrical groupings. A mosaic displaying an unswept dining room floor must have served as an admonition to careless diners (as did messages painted on a dining room wall urging them to behave themselves respectably during the meal—such as are found in the House of the Moralist). Equally startling is the depiction of a fight between an octopus and a lobster, intended for the floor of a pool or a bath. Mosaics were also beginning to creep up from the floors to the walls and vaults upon which, centuries later, they were to become Byzantium's most characteristic art. In the niches adorning fountains in Pompeian courtyards, they must have produced scintillating effects in the strong sunshine.

The largest houses of all, known as "villas," were not inside the town itself, but in the surrounding countryside, where they provided rich men and women with luxury summer residences, with ample farms attached. The Villa of Publius Fannius Sinistor at Boscoreale has soaring architectural vistas, and the Villa of the Mysteries has long been known for an extraordinary cycle of religious wall paintings connected with the Dionysiac rite; while the Villa of the Papyri, outside Herculaneum (imaginatively reconstructed as the J. Paul Getty Museum at Malibu in California), became famous for its astonishing yields both of literary papyri and ancient bronze statues. Recent researches have added enormously to the number of known villas throughout this entire area, so that they form one of the most active and productive fields of current study. For example, more than a dozen such mansions have come to light on the maritime hillside above Stabiae (Castellamare di Stabia), some three miles south of Pompeii. And now a very imposing villa, with substantial farm buildings and lands, has been discovered at Oplontis or Oplontiae (Torre Annunziata), three miles west of Pompeii; more than fifty of its rooms have been cleared, and a long, continuous colonnade facing south over the seashore. As happened in so many cases, extensive damage was caused to the villa by the earthquake of A.D. 62. Then, seventeen years later, the disastrous eruption buried the house under six feet of ash and pumice, topped by another fifteen of volcanic mud.

There is clearly more, much more, still to be found at these country villas. But indeed the same applies to Pompeii as a whole; two-fifths of the place remains to be discovered. Fortunately, excavation continues unabated. There have been notable recent discoveries not only at Stabiae, Oplontis and Herculaneum, but also in the central Pompeian zone itself, for instance at a vineyard just inside the walls of the town, in a necropolis in the outskirts, and at a number of the city's town houses as well, including those of Sallust (so-called) and Gaius Julius Polybius. The house of the latter, who owned inns and hotels in the city, has continued to yield finds of particular importance, including shortly before these lines were written, a collection of bronzes (among them, a notable statue of a young man), which is one of the most significant discoveries of recent years.

So let us hope that the red bowels of Vesuvius will not become aggressively explosive once again. It is not possible to be too optimistic on this point. Every month, the local observatory registers up to ten *microterremoti,* mini-earthquakes. Moreover, since A.D. 79, there have been no less than seventy eruptions—averaging one every twenty-seven years. The last of them took place in 1944, thirty-five years ago. It served as a reminder that the mountain was the only active volcano on the continent of Europe—and will someday, therefore, be heard of again, although the pause since the last outburst has been a long one. Moreover, when the next eruption comes, it is unlikely to be a negligible affair. The 1944 disturbance sealed the top of the crater down completely, removing the plume or pall of smoke which in many paintings of Vesuvius is shown hanging over the mountain. Next time, therefore, the seething underneath the earth will remain bottled up until the whole top is blown violently off, just as it was blown off in A.D. 79. As the novelist Charles Dickens declared, "the mountain is the genius of the scene, the doom and destiny of this beautiful country, biding its time."

Note. For readers who feel strong enough for a recipe for Pompeian fish-sauce, *(garum)* I repeat the version offered in my *Cities of Vesuvius.* "The entrails of sprats or sardines—the parts that could not be used for salting—were mixed with finely chopped portions of fish, and with roe and eggs, and a warm room and beaten into a homogeneous pulp until it fermented. When this *liquamen,* as it was called, had been much reduced over a period of six weeks by evaporation, it was placed in a basket with a perforated bottom through which the residue filtered slowly down into a receptacle. This end-product, decanted into jars, was the famous *garum;* the dregs left over, also regarded as edible, were known as *allec.*"

Michael Grant

16

THE CITY:
PUBLIC BUILDINGS
AND OCCUPATIONS

vehicles to pass, and pedestrians to cross without walking in the drainage water.
(p. 24, 26–27).

MURAL INSCRIPTIONS.
One of the most interesting and vivid documents that Pompeii has preserved of the daily life of antiquity is the network of mural inscriptions found on practically all the walls of the city. Painted or merely scratched on both the exterior and interior walls of homes, shops and public buildings, these brief

inscriptions are often only political slogans inciting the electors to vote for a particular candidate, who was generally the proprietor of the house itself. Or perhaps they are simply vulgar insults or obscene allusions to prostitutes (sometimes even with an indication of price), or words of encouragement for a particular gladiator, or reminiscences of happy or unhappy love affairs. One amorous inscription, perhaps a fragment of a lost lyric, reads: "The soul is accustomed to take what is due it and to bestow. If you follow this habit, Venus will grant our wishes and her benevolence will make us rich."

One of the many ELECTORAL INSCRIPTIONS found on the walls of Pompeii. They were written in red or black capitals by professional notice painters.

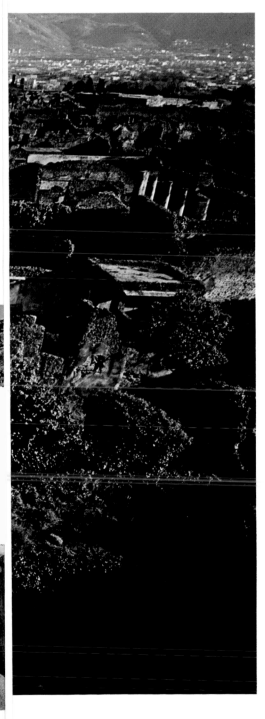

VIEW OF POMPEII FROM THE TOWER OF MERCURY looking toward the Forum along Mercury Street.

21

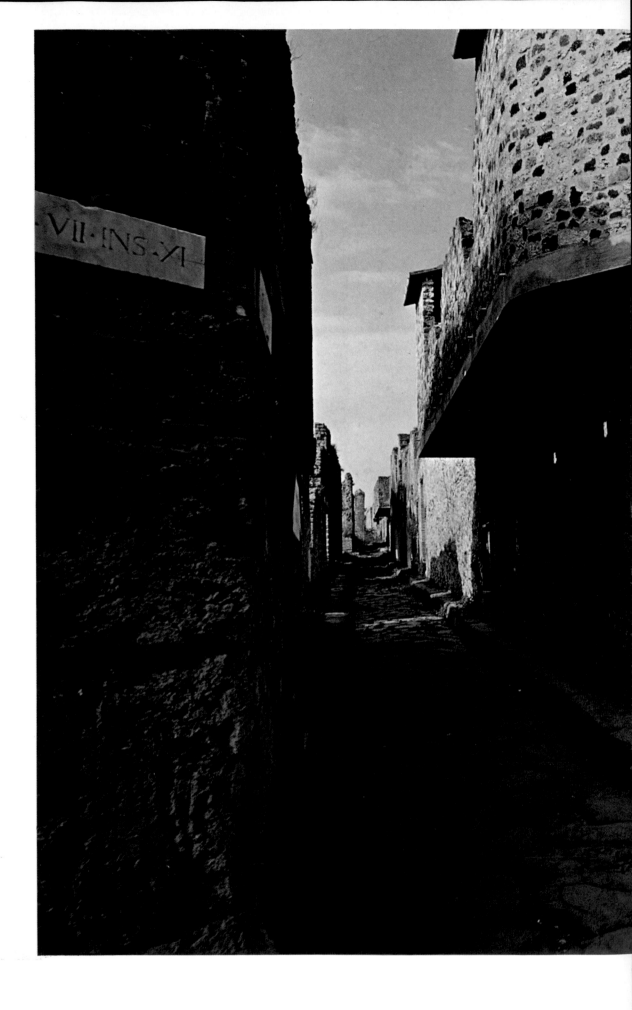

Left
AMPHORA WITH PUTTI, detail
Blue glass; 12⅝".
The technique of this amphora—showing putti
harvesting grapes—is similar to that of cameos.
Dating from the second quarter of the 1st
century A.D., it was probably not produced in
Pompeii, where craftsmanship did not reach
this level.
From a tomb on the Via dei Sepolcri,
Pompeii.
Naples, National Archaeological Museum

Right
A TOMB built against the walls between the
Herculaneum and Vesuvian Gates. Such tombs
were often small versions of edifices of the
period.

Right
TOMB IN THE NECROPOLIS OUTSIDE
THE NUCERIAN GATE. In two of the
upper niches are the busts of a man and a
woman. The three inscriptions on white
marble slabs commemorate Publius Flavius
Philoxenus, freedman of Publius, and Flavia
Agathea, freedwoman of Publius.

THE AMPHITHEATER AND THE GREAT PALAESTRA

As in all Greek and, later, Roman cities great importance was given in Pompeii to public spectacles which involved the mass participation of the inhabitants. The public buildings erected for these activities were built in two distinct areas along the axis of the Via dell'Abbondanza. One was near its eastern end and consisted of the Amphitheater (pp. 32–33) and the Great Palaestra; the other was close to the Doric Temple on the Triangular Forum and was made up of the two theaters and other buildings.

The Amphitheater was reserved for the shows of the gladiators and the boxers, horse racing, fights between animals and between men and wild beasts (bulls, boars and bears). It was an exclusively Roman type of edifice. Elliptical in form, it had a central area completely surrounded by tiered seats for the spectators. The outer structure consists of high arches which are further supported by four sets of wide stairs leading to the upper galleries. The Amphitheater, built around 70 B.C., could hold between eighteen and twenty thousand people: the entire population of the city (about 15,000) plus the inhabitants of the surrounding villages and the countryside.

The Great Palaestra, constructed during the reign of Augustus, was built to give the young men of the city a place to practice their various sports. In accordance with the Emperor's instructions, the youths were grouped into associations which not only organized the training of the athletes and their preparation for the games but also supplied a form of obviously imperialistic, political education. The Palaestra was a grandiose rectangular construction (463 by 351 feet) surrounded by century-old sycamores, which had, together with various sanitary facilities, an interior portico and, in the center, an open area with a swimming pool. The latter was very similar to its modern counterparts: 113 feet long, 82 feet wide; and an inclined bottom with a minimum depth of 3¼ feet and a maximum depth of 8½ feet.

A precious pictorial document of these edifices survives in the mural painting, *Brawl in the Amphitheater* (left), in which the Palaestra can be seen on the right, the Amphitheater on the left and two watchtowers of the city walls in the background. This fresco depicts the quarrel which exploded in 59 A.D. between the inhabitants of Pompeii and those of Nuceria. It was reportedly caused by rival enthusiasms aroused by the gladiatorial games and ended with many dead and injured. More probably the rivalry resulted from the Emperor Nero having two years before assigned to Nuceria a part of Pompeian territory. This political explanation can be confirmed by the fact that Nero and the Roman senate ordered the Amphitheater closed for ten years.

BRAWL IN THE AMPHITHEATER
Mural painting: 66⅞" × 72⅞".
The painting shows the structure of the Amphitheater with its arches and stairs. From House of the Gladiator Actius Anecetus.
Naples, National Archaeological Museum

Pp. 32–33
The Arena and the tiered spectator seats of the AMPHITHEATER. Built around 70 B.C. by the duumviri Gaius Quinctius Valgus and Marcus Porcius, it is the earliest amphitheater known. An inscription indicates that it was dedicated to Roman colonists.

THE ODEUM, or Small Theater, was built in
the first years of the Roman colony by the
same duumviri who built the Amphitheater.

Pp. 36–37
REHEARSAL FOR A GREEK SATYR
PLAY
Mosaic emblema; 22⅞" × 23¼".
The seated bald man is directing the actors in
steps to the music played by the figure with
pipes. At right, one actor is donning a
costume.
From Pompeii, House of the Tragic Poet.
Naples, National Archaeological Museum

SCENE FROM A COMEDY
Terracotta relief; 17¾" × 20⅞".
One of the few known depictions of the comic
genre, this scene from a play exemplifies the
lively mimic acting of Roman comedy,
especially in the roles of servants and old
people.
From the Farnese Collection.
Naples, National Archaeological Museum

One of the ATLANTES decorating the
entrance to the Odeum. Made of tufa, the
kneeling figure supports a cornice on which
there were decorative elements.

THE THEATERS.

Pompeii's two theaters—the Great Theater and the Odeum (covered theater)—were part of an original urban center erected on the slopes and top of a ridge running to the sea. This included the Doric Temple (6th century B.C., perhaps the most ancient of the Pompeian sanctuaries), the Samnite Palaestra (2nd century B.C. and probably the headquarters of a political-military association), the Temple of Isis (p. 53) and the Temple of Jupiter Meilichius (3rd–2nd century B.C.).

The Great Theater can be dated from between the 3rd and 2nd centuries B.C., and had a capacity of at least 5,000 spectators. It has the characteristic Greek-Hellenistic form of a horseshoe closed at the open end by a rectangular platform—the *proscenium* on which the actors performed—and a wall with three openings. This wall—the *scenae frons*—decorated with columns and movable painted scenery—served as a background for the action and permitted the entrance and exit of the performers. Outside Greece, tragedy was usually presented for a cultural elite, and this theater, therefore, probably offered

35

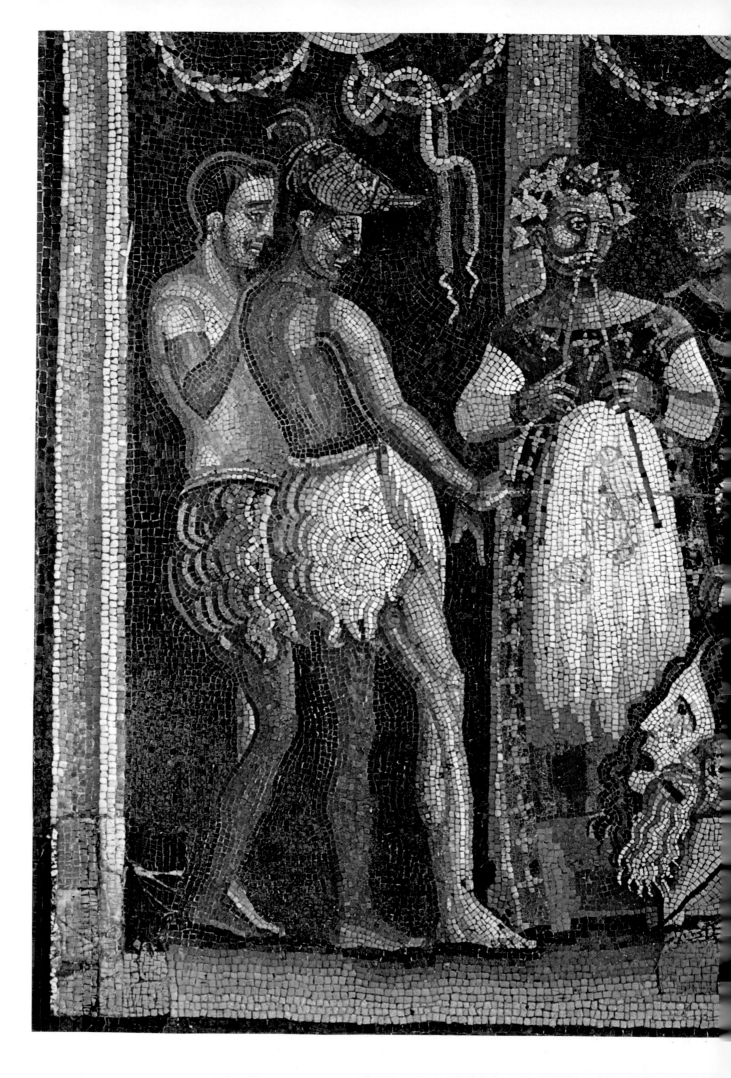

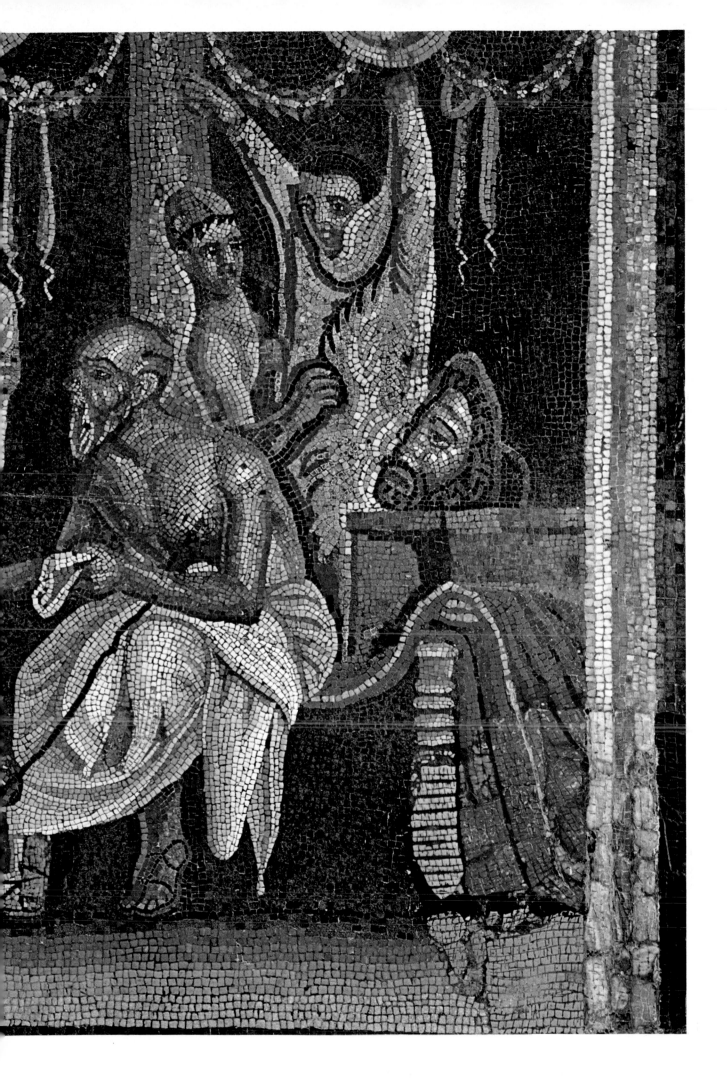

CHARIOT RACE
Mural painting; 22½" × 36¼".
The painting—incomplete at the top—shows four *quadrigae* (four-horse chariots) in the arena. Chariot racing and gladiator combats were the most popular sports in the Roman era.
From Pompeii, House of the Chariots (?).
Naples, National Archaeological Museum

mostly comedies and satiric dramas or parodies of tragedy enlivened by the vivacious choreography of musicians, mimes and dancers in bizarre costumes (pp. 35, 159). During the Roman era the most popular spectacles were farces improvised on scenarios that accentuated the grotesque aspects of the comedies. There was also mime, characterized by actors who performed without masks (the only ones to do so in ancient times) and by brief comic scenes drawn from daily life that were often obscene, contained political allusions, and were interspersed with strip-teases, songs and dances (p 35).

On the other hand, the Odeum (p. 34) was designed for music and recitations, and was therefore of limited dimensions. Although similar to the other theater in its semicircular form and structure, it was provided with a permanent roof for acoustical reasons. It was built about 80 B.C., alongside the Great Theater.

Behind the Great Theater and the Odeum there is a large peristyle called the "Quadriporticus" (p. 40), consisting of a large, rectangular open area surrounded on all sides by a covered colonnade which offered shelter and various conveniences for the public during the long intermissions. This structure dates back to the Samnite era, but after the earthquake of 62 A.D. it was converted into barracks for the gladiators. An apartment was set aside for the trainer and several rooms were probably reserved as lodgings for travelling gladiators and their families. Richly decorated armor and costumes embroidered in gold which have been found in the excavations must have served the combatants for their choreographic parades in the Amphitheater that preceded the fighting (p. 41).

Right
SCENE FROM A TRAGEDY
Mural painting
In addition to the masks, the actors of Roman tragedy wore the high laced boots called *cothurni,* to make them more imposing and enhance the solemnity of their acting.
From Pompeii, House of the Dioscuri.
Naples, National Archaeological Museum

Left
The DORIC PORTICO, also called the QUADRIPORTICUS, was built in the 2nd century B.C. behind the Great Theatre, as a shelter for spectators between the acts. After the earthquake of 62 A.D., it was adapted for gladiators and their servants. Many beautiful gladiatorial weapons have been found there.

THE FORUM.

The forum in classical antiquity was the large square in which the commercial, political and religious life of the ancient cities evolved. Propitiously situated, it was the place where the population gathered to buy and sell its products and around which the city developed. The Greeks and Romans, whether they founded a new city or settled in a pre-existing town, conceived the forum as the veritable administrative center containing all the public buildings needed for the life of the city as well as the temples dedicated to the most important divinities. And they imposed on all the structures a homogeneous architectonic standard.

The Forum in Pompeii, one of the finest in the Graeco-Roman world, was distinguished by the sober elegance of the public buildings around it and the order with which they were laid out. The square—465 feet long by 125 feet wide,

A fighting HELMET decorated with the Roman eagle. Bronze grilles protected the eyes, and on the back, a flange covered the neck.

41

surrounded on three sides by a two-storied colonnade, of which only a few columns remain—was the place where the shopkeepers and itinerant peddlers carried on their trade on market days. In front of the colonnade was a series of equestrian statues of magistrates and important citizens. The square was kept clear of vehicular traffic by being raised two steps above street level; and merchandise was loaded and unloaded in the side alleys between the public buildings, with the result that the Pompeians had the entire area at their disposal for their business affairs, political meetings and religious ceremonies.

At the southern end of the Forum were to be found the five buildings in which the political and civil activities of the population took place (p. 43). In the month of March each year the freemen of the city gathered in the Comitium—a simple quadrangular edifice—to elect four officials: two Aediles or superintendents of commerce and public works and games; and two Duumviri, the highest officials, who acted as judges and promulgated the laws enacted by the municipal council of senators (the so-called Decuriones). The duumviri probably had their offices in a small building on the south side of the Forum, with the city's archives in an adjoining building. The senators were elected or appointed from among the members of the Pompeian upper classes—usually landowners—and served for life. The senatorial council meetings were held in the *Curia,* a structure that flanked the Archives building on the west.

The Pompeian FORUM—one of the most complete in existence—was built in Samnite times, in the second half of the 2nd century B.C. It was severely damaged in the earthquake of 62 A.D., and its reconstruction was still under way at the moment of the eruption.

PRESENTATION AT THE FORUM
Mural painting.
An important moment in the life of a young
Roman citizen was his initiation into public life
in the presentation ceremony at the Forum,
which is the subject of this painting.

The interior of THE BASILICA, at the southwest end of the Forum. This building was the center for commercial transactions and law administration. From its style and structure, it can be dated from the late 2nd century B.C. Discovery of tiles of Oscan manufacture, which covered the roof, seem to indicate construction around 130 B.C.

THE BASILICA.

Lawsuits and trials took place in the Basilica, where, in addition, arrangements could be made with lawyers and important business transacted. Begun in the second half of the second century B.C., contemporaneously with the redesigning and reconstruction of the Forum, the Basilica of Pompeii is one of the oldest and finest examples of this distinctively Roman type of structure that was to serve later as a model for the churches of the early Christians. It was a vast, rectangular, roofed building—230 feet long—with a central hall surrounded by a colonnade from which the public could follow the proceedings. At one end a tribunal was erected for the judges and magistrates.

The temples of the Forum were dedicated to the most important divinities of Olympus: Jupiter Capitoline (2nd century B.C.); the public *Lares,* the tutelary gods of the city (1st century A.D.); the Emperor Vespasian, who had contributed extensively to the relief of the city after the earthquake of 62 A.D.; and Apollo, guardian divinity of Pompeii up to the time of the Roman conquest. The temple dedicated to Apollo that we see today was built in the 2nd century B.C. but it was constructed over the ruins of a sanctuary dating from the sixth century B.C. (p. 45).

THE MACELLUM.

The *Macellum*—the large roofed market reserved for the sale of farm produce—was a building common to all the cities of Greece, Asia Minor and North Africa. In Pompeii it was constructed in the northeast corner of the

Forum during the second century B.C. and was extensively rebuilt and enlarged after the earthquake of 62 A.D. (p. 46). It was square and had regular rows of both open-air and indoor shops; in the center of the courtyard there was an enclosed octagonal area with a fountain in which the fish were cleaned. The walls of the shops were decorated with paintings depicting mythological scenes and still-lifes (p. 47).

On the opposite side of the Forum was the Olitorius Forum, consisting of a portico where cereals and dried legumes—which together with fish were the basic elements of the Pompeian diet—were traded. Public weights and measures, controlled by magistrates, had been introduced for the regulation of purchases and sales; those in Pompeii were installed in a recess in the wall enclosing the court of the Temple of Apollo, probably in the first century B.C. They consisted of two slabs of limestone with a total of twelve cavities corresponding to twelve different measures. There was a hole in the bottom for the release of the weighed commodities.

The TEMPLE OF APOLLO, flanking the western side of the Forum. The temple was built in the 2nd century B.C. on the ruins of a 6th-century sanctuary, but appears to have been restored after the earthquake of 62 B.C.

Trade in wool in Pompeii was most probably carried on in its largest building, the Eumachia, on the east side of the Forum. This structure was built about 22 A.D. by Eumachia, a wealthy noblewoman who was the proprietor of various concerns involved in both the wine and wool trades as well as the production of terracotta jars. She was also the high priestess of Venus, the tutelary divinity of the city during the period of the Roman domination.

The building consisted of a large internal courtyard surrounded by a colonnade and on three sides by a wide corridor illuminated by windows. Four niches in the facade contained statues; most probably two of the recesses were occupied by the auctioneer and a banker when there were important public sales. Given the plan of the edifice the hypothesis has been put forward that, rather than a commodities exchange, it was the headquarters and general warehouse of the wool industry's merchants and workers, the weavers, washers, and dyers.

THE PUBLIC BATHS.
Pompeii had no fewer than four public baths of large proportions. They were richly decorated with stucco reliefs (p. 49) and mural paintings, which indicates the importance of those public facilities in the daily life of the population. Only rarely, in fact, could anyone have the luxury of a private bath in his home, given the frequent scarcity of water. The oldest baths were the Stabian Thermae which can be dated from the 4th century B.C. although they were rebuilt in the 2nd century B.C. contemporaneously with others near the Forum (p. 48). The Sarno

The forehall of THE MACELLUM, the food market at the northwest corner of the Forum. In a row behind the columns are the bases which once supported statues.

ULYSSES RECOGNIZED BY PENELOPE,
a painting in the Fourth Style decorating the
northwest wall of the Macellum.

Bronze SHOPKEEPER'S SCALES of simple
design found in the excavations at Pompeii.

and Central Thermae (begun after 62 A.D. and never finished) were also located
in the center of the city and served a wealthy residential area.

The bathing facilities were laid out around a large colonnaded courtyard which
with its swimming pool served also as a gymnasium for physical training. Two
distinct but similar sections were reserved respectively for the women and the
men. Each contained: a *frigidarium,* the swimming pool with cold water; the
tepidarium, a room with circulating hot air, a kind of prototype of the modern
sauna; the *caldarium,* with tubs of boiling water and scorching circulating air
heated in special furnaces.

The hot-water room (*caldarium*) of the
FORUM BATHS. The round marble basin
(*labrum*) at the apse-shaped end of the room
contained cold water for rubbing down. The
tub for hot baths (*alveus*) was at the opposite
end. Floor and walls are hollow for the
passage of hot air.

Right
The myth of Ganymede abducted by an eagle
is depicted in this STUCCO DECORATION
on a vault of the Stabian Baths. This art form,
also used in the decoration of private houses,
reached a high level of development in
Pompeii and Herculaneum during the last
years before the eruption.

CULTS AND DIVINITIES.

In the Graeco-Roman world religion was fundamentally either a personal cult of a divinity to whom propitiatory gifts were offered in order to obtain his or her benevolence, or it was the totality of the citizenry organizing solemn processions and the sacrifice of animals on certain days of the year in the honor of one or another of the more important divinities—Jupiter, Juno, Minerva—with the hope of securing the protection of the city. In Southern Italy the majority of the population, being employed in agricultural activities, sacrificed to Ceres, goddess of growing vegetation and the fruits of the earth. Pompeii in particular, when it became a Roman colony in 80 B.C., was placed under the protection of Venus to whom the dictator Sulla was especially devoted.

The temples, therefore, were authorized to accommodate only the statues of the divinities to whom they were dedicated and below which the offerings were placed (p. 51). There was not even a priesthood inasmuch as the latter's functions were performed by prominent citizens elected for these services by the citizens or by the augurs of haruspices who knew how to interpret the will of the gods on the basis of the entrails of the sacrificed animals.

At the time of his reorganization of the state, Octavianus Augustus, imitating the Middle Eastern states, introduced the imperial cult. The Temple of Fortuna Augusta, the goddess of good fortune and protectress of the emperor, was built in Pompeii in 3 B.C. by a certain Marcus Tullius, an important magistrate, a particular favorite of Augustus, and a member of a branch of Cicero's family.

TEMPLE OF ISIS.

During the Hellenistic period several cults of Middle Eastern and Egyptian

SISTRUMS AND CYMBALS found in the Temple of Isis. The sistrum, a bronze loop crossed by rods producing a tinkling sound, was shaken by worshippers of Isis during rituals. The cymbals, beaten rhythmically, were also played during religious ceremonies. From Pompeii, Temple of Isis. Naples, National Archaeological Museum.

Right
AN OFFERING TO BACCHUS
Mural painting.
The cult of Dionysus-Bacchus was widespread in Southern Italy, where the god was identified with the old Italic deity Liber.

Right
THE TEMPLE OF ISIS. Stairs lead up to the pronaos and to a narrow, rectangular cella. Before the temple are an altar and the Purgatorium, a small building where water from the Nile was kept for purification rituals.

Left
SMALL TEMPLE WITH OFFERING SCENE
Mural painting.
In this detail from a panel in the Fourth Style, the statue of a divinity can be seen in the pronaos of a small temple. At the right of the temple, people are making offerings at an altar.
From Pompeii.
Naples, National Archaeological Museum

origin spread into Italy, particularly on the popular level; they were based on mystical rites reserved to the initiated few and they promised a better future life. One of the most important of these was the cult of Isis which, beginning in the 3rd century B.C., combined certain aspects of the occult ceremonies of the Isis faith with the esoteric cult of the Greek goddess Demeter. The new religion was particularly opposed by Rome.

In Pompeii the Temple of Isis had already been built by the end of the 2nd century B.C. behind the Great Theater (above). Destroyed in the earthquake of 62 A.D. it was immediately reconstructed, nominally at the expense of Numerius Popidius Celsius, then a child of six. By this act of the infant's father—an extremely wealthy freedman enriched by trade but excluded from public life by his servile origins, the doors of the most exclusive society were opened to his son, and he was rewarded with a seat in the Senate.

The edifice consisted of a large colonnaded courtyard that contained a small temple with images of Egyptian divinities, a large open-air altar for the sacrifices, a well and a square outbuilding with a subterranean crypt where the initiated purified themselves with water from the Nile brought from Egypt in special jars. Behind the colonnade there were two halls whose function is not precisely known; but the largest was probably reserved for the performance of religious spectacles or plays.

LOCAL INDUSTRIES.

From the very beginning Pompeii had a flourishing economy which permitted it to maintain a local production sufficient for its fundamental needs without recourse to imports. The cereals, fruits and vegetables were all raised in the surrounding countryside and amply covered the needs of the population, which supplemented its basic diet with fish or pork and lamb brought in from the interior. Objects for daily use—ceramics, glass, bronze, and wood—were produced by the local artisans who also supplied luxury articles for the richer inhabitants.

The real wealth of Pompeii, as of the other cities of Campania, can be attributed to the export of wine and olive oil, inasmuch as the surrounding terrain and the slopes of Vesuvius were extraordinarily fertile and adaptable for the cultivation of vineyards and olive trees (as they still are today). The fortunes of the great noble families—the Eumachii and the Holconii—were built up on the basis of exports of wine, which over a period of more than two centuries extended as far as Gaul and North Africa. Another export item was cloth produced from the wool of the sheep raised in the mountains of Samnium and Lucania; it was woven and dyed in the numerous workshops of the *fullones,* as the workers of the wool industry were called.

There also existed in Pompeii several shipping companies which generally operated along the sea lanes leading forth from the small port at the mouth of the Sarnus, a river passing near the city. The wine and oil were stored and shipped in terracotta jars and amphorae that were produced in small family-owned kilns.

WORKSHOPS.

It can only be surmised, in view of the lack of precise archeological proof, that there must have been numerous small firms of builders of private housing and workshops of painters, mosaicists and stuccoers who must have been very active after the earthquake of 62 A.D. in the work of reconstruction.

In accordance with a widespread custom in the Mediterranean area retail sales were made not only by peddlers but also in the houses of the shopkeepers themselves. The latter reserved the upper story for family use and installed on the ground floor their warerooms and sales counters which could be seen directly from the street. If they personally produced certain goods, the workrooms were also on the ground floor and were laid out around an inner courtyard. In the case here illustrated (p. 56) the baker had installed not only his brick oven but also his granite millstones, the animals that turned the mill, and the wells for the water needed for his dough.

TAVERNS.

Especially in the area between the theaters and the Amphitheater there were many taverns (*cauponae*) that sold and served hot dishes and wine. Holes were made in the counter to hold the egg-shaped amphorae and there was also an opening for the braziers used for heating the water with which the wine was diluted. The upper floor with a few rooms and a latrine was often used as a hotel or brothel. The walls were decorated with small mediocre paintings that at times were obscene; we can also find spontaneous sketches of barroom scenes drawn by the customers (p. 61).

The *thermopolia,* which served mulled wine, were more elegant, and in addition to drinks often offered their patrons the services of a true restaurant; their dining

EMBLEMA WITH THE SYMBOLS OF LIFE AND DEATH
Mosaic; 18½″ × 16½″.
This emblema was found in the *triclinium* of the Tannery. The skull is surmounted by a square; and below are a butterfly and a wheel—symbolizing respectively the instability of life and the chances of Fortune.

The facade of two TEXTILE WORKSHOPS (*textrinae*). Graffiti inscribed on the wall indicate that the looms were on the floor above, and the goods sold in the shops below.

The interior of a DYERS' WORKSHOP, with
a large dyeing tank in the center.

Below
THE BAKERY
Mural painting; 24″ × 20⅞″.
The painting represents the free distribution of
bread during elections. The loaves are
identical with some found in the excavations.
From Pompeii.
Naples, National Archaeological Museum.

56

rooms, the *triclinia,* were decorated with great refinement (p. 60). In addition to the indoor rooms there were often open-air *triclinia* in the garden, covered by a grape arbor behind the house. The receipts of a day's business were found in one of these restaurants: 683 sesterces, a respectable sum when one bears in mind that a tunic cost only fifteen.

METAL CRAFTS AND JEWELRY.

In the Republican period and the early years of the Empire Campania enjoyed a certain position of importance in the production of bronze and silver objects. Bronze was employed for household articles such as small stoves (p. 78), lamps and braziers; silver, in view of its rarity, was considered throughout the ancient world to be the most precious metal and was used for only the most elegant table services (p. 61). Decorative objects such as statuettes for the house and garden were generally of bronze; religious furnishings—vases, tripods for sacrificial

Right
The sales counter of A POMPEIAN THERMOPOLIUM, a shop selling hot food and drinks. Food containers were fitted into the round openings of the counter. At the far end, to the right, is the shrine of the Lares. Below the figures are two serpents, representing the tutelary spirits of the house.

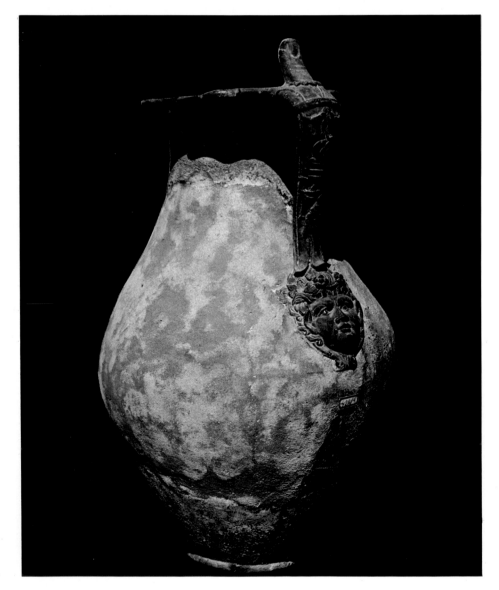

Left
BRONZE AMPHORA with decorated handle. Although Pompeii was not a major center for bronzework, there was a good level of craftsmanship there.
From Pompeii.
Naples, National Archaeological Museum

P. 60
One of the frescoed walls of the THERMOPOLIUM ON VIA DELL'ABBONDANZA. The small picture on the wall to the left represents *Europa and the Bull.*

P. 61
ARGUMENT IN A CAUPONA (TAVERN) Mural painting.
The man standing near the table seems to be arguing with the seated one, who is drinking. The other two men, probably waiters, intervene to settle the quarrel.
From Pompeii, the Caupona on Mercury Street.
Naples, National Archaeological Museum.

P. 61
SILVERWARE from Pompeii and sites in the Vesuvian area. The plate and bowl have handles decorated with foliage and birds' heads.
Naples, National Archaeological Museum.

THETIS IN VULCAN'S WORKSHOP, detail
Mural painting.
A metal craftsman at work, hammering a
design on a helmet.
Naples, National Archaeological Museum

fires, offering plates—could also be made of silver, the choice depending on the wealth of the donor.

Even if Pompeii in this type of production did not have the importance of Capua, which was famous, above all, for the manufacture of bronze objects, in which the great Pompeian families also invested, the city had a large but indeterminate number of silversmiths and bronze casters capable of satisfying the needs of the population.

The arts of the goldsmith and the gem and cameo cutter for the production of jewelry for personal use were also practiced at a rather high technical level. One of the most interesting finds was the discovery of the work tools and box of stones of the jeweler Pinarius Cerialis. There were one hundred and fourteen precious gems and stones including amethysts, agate, carnelian, and sardonyx still in a rough or semifinished stage; twenty-eight had been cut and polished, thus giving us a complete picture of the phases of the jeweler's operations.

THE PRIVATE HOUSES
AND THEIR ART

VILLA AT THE SEASIDE
Mural painting; diameter 9⅞".
A splendid *villa maritima* with columns
running the whole length of the facade; in
front are two jetties projecting into the sea.
Back of the house are trees and buildings.
From Stabiae.
Naples, National Archaeological Museum

THE POMPEIAN HOUSE.

Approximately sixty percent of the buildings of Pompeii have been brought to
light in two and one-half centuries of excavations, the majority of which are
dwellings. Pompeii, like Herculaneum, therefore constitutes a priceless document for a knowledge of daily life in ancient times, even if its houses offer some
characteristics that were peculiar to the Campanian region, or at least to the
seacoast. The mild winters with an abundance of light and sun, long middle
seasons and very hot summers permitted a large part of domestic life to be
carried on in the open air, in surroundings linked by porticoes or in the gardens
of even the most modest dwellings.

The poorest houses were very simple. If the proprietors were small shopkeepers
their counters were on the ground floor with the family rooms and kitchen
behind them, or on a mezzanine built above the shop, known as the *pergula*. The
freedmen and artisans generally lived in houses with rooms built around a small
inner courtyard called the *xystus,* and a tiny garden called the *viridarium.* Such
houses were decorated with paintings and mosaics which, although very simple,
were often rather elegant. Like the residences of the wealthier citizens, these
houses were occupied by single families in accordance with a custom common to
all Mediterranean civilizations; only after the earthquake of 62 A.D. and the
resulting shortage of housing were some of the largest buildings subdivided into
apartments.

The typical house of Pompeii—a city inhabited for the most part by wealthy
merchants, bankers, lawyers and landowners with swarms of servants—was an
elegant residence rationally laid out, the basic elements of which were the

A LARGE SEASIDE VILLA
Mural painting; 6⅔″ × 15½″.
This example of the architectural paintings decorating the walls of many houses in Pompeii gives an idea of the elaborate "maritime villas" built along the coast of the Bay of Naples, none of which have survived.
From Stabiae.
Naples, National Archaeological Museum

Pp. 66–67
LANDSCAPE WITH VILLA BY THE SEA
Mural painting.
Reflected in these depictions of seaside residences is the appreciation Romans had for the beauty of nature. Typical of such scenes are the figures sketched in the foreground.
Pompeii, House of Marcus Lucretius Fronto.

atrium, the *tablinum* or living room, and the peristyle or garden courtyard.

The *atrium* was a large rectangular room with an opening in the roof—the *compluvium*—directly above the *impluvium,* or pool in the pavement below, designed to collect rain water for the needs of the household. (p. 86–87). The overhang of the roof rested on beams or columns. After the construction of Augustus' aqueduct the *atrium* had the sole function of a reception hall for the daily business of the owner and was simply furnished with stools and a marble table on which ancestral portraits in wax or stone were displayed.

The *tablinum,* situated between the *atrium* and the peristyle, was usually richly decorated with paintings. It could be used both as a living room and the bedchamber of the owners, and could be closed off, like the other rooms of the house, by curtains. The peristyle was an inner courtyard of ample proportions surrounded by a roofed colonnade and decorated with plants, statues and a pool. The bedrooms of the family and servants (slaves or freedmen with their families), the kitchen and the other facilities were laid out in rows along the two sides, beginning from the *atrium* and extending along the peristyle. From the 2nd century B.C. on, two new types of rooms were created around the peristyle in imitation of the Greek-Hellenistic architecture of the eastern Mediterranean: a dining room, i.e. the *triclinium,* and a reception or banquet hall, i.e. the *oecus.* These were sumptuously decorated with mural paintings and mosaic floors. At times even more than one *triclinium* was built with the aim of exploiting various locations according to the seasonal variations of the temperature. In some cases they consisted of small pavilions erected in the larger gardens.

65

A SANCTUARY NEAR THE SEA, detail
Mural painting; 20½" × 24⅜".
Quite conventional is the composition of this
scene: a small circular temple (*tholos*) flanked
by porticoes, a landscape with trees and
buildings in the background, a terrace with
figures, the sea crossed by boats. More
unusual is the seated woman playing with a
dog.
From Pompeii.
Naples, National Archaeological Museum.

In the Hellenistic period it became customary to add galleries and "pseudo-porticoes" (long, closed corridors with barrel-vaulted roofing) around the garden in the rear of the house, which were used as storerooms. A floor was often added over the *atrium* for additional family rooms; and this in turn permitted the installation of a private bath with basins and stoves in the area of the peristyle. Shops were opened in the facade and the slaves or freedmen were entrusted with the sale of merchandise or agricultural products.

Pompeian houses, even if they were built on this basic plan, were, nevertheless, characterized by extraordinary variety in their proportions and in the arrangement of individual elements. One must not forget that the oldest homes date from the end of the 5th and the beginning of the 4th centuries B.C. and that these were still occupied at the moment of the eruption of Vesuvius. During the centuries, therefore, they were continously being enlarged and reconstructed, thus acquiring individual characteristics.

We can also presume that, at least as far as the houses of the wealthier citizens were concerned, attempts were made to copy the magnificent decorations of the luxurious villas that the rich Romans were beginning to build on the seashore of

Right
GARDEN PAVILION, detail
Mural painting; 8' × 4'1".
Some of the finest architectural paintings that
have come down to us are from the country
house of a member of the imperial family.
This detail shows a pavilion in the garden of a
villa; on the right is a column surmounted by
the protective divinity of the house.
From Boscotrecase, Villa of Agrippa
Posthumus.
Naples, National Archaeological Museum.

the Bay of Naples, the Amalfi coast, and on the islands of Ischia and Capri from the 1st century B.C. onward. We have some information about these "maritime villas," those of Tiberius on Capri, and of Pliny—who described the eruption of Vesuvius—in Misenum. However, the pictorial representations of them found in the mural paintings in the houses of Pompeii, Herculaneum and Stabiae are probably considerably idealized (pp. 64, 65).

THE DANCING SATYR, called
THE DANCING FAUN
Bronze; 30¾".
Often erroneously referred to as a faun—after
which the house was named—the statue was
found near the impluvium of the main atrium
and is thought to be the original decoration of
the pool.
From Pompeii, House of the Faun.
Naples, National Archaeological Museum.

The main atrium of the HOUSE OF THE FAUN; in the center of the *impluvium* is a cast of the original statue of the *Dancing Faun*.

Pp. 72-73
THE BATTLE OF ISSUS
Mosaio; 8' 10¾" × 16' 9⅝".
This large mosaic, made of very small tesserae, originally decorated the floor of the exedra in the House of the Faun. It is a copy of a Greek painting of the 4th century B.O., probably by the Greek painter Philoxenos of Eretria. Defeated by Alexander, Darius flees from the battlefield on his chariot, turning back and looking towards the Macedonian king, portrayed at the left.
From Pompeii, House of the Faun.
Naples, National Archaeological Museum

HOUSE OF THE FAUN.

One of the most beautiful residences of Pompeii—and of all antiquity—is the House of the Faun, named after a bronze statue of a dancing "faun" (p. 70) which decorated the pool of the main atrium. The house is enormous—approximately 32,000 square feet—built at the beginning of the 2nd century B.C., and is believed to have belonged to Publius Cornelius Sulla, nephew of the Roman dictator Sulla who, after 80 B.C., was assigned the task of governing Pompeii as a Roman colony. This house was similar to those of the largest Hellenistic cities and was certainly most luxurious for it contained two atria, two peristyles, two dining rooms, and an extraordinary number of rooms and small, but exceptionally well organized hygienic facilities. Most of the stuccoes that decorated the columns and walls—still visible when excavation was begun (1830–1832)—are lost, but practically all the mosaic pavements with their geometric patterns, animals, Nilotic landscapes and marine creatures are still preserved, either in loco or in the Archaeological Museum of Naples.

The magnificent mosaic of the *Battle of Issus* from the House of the Faun,

Left
WOMEN CONSULTING A SORCERESS
Mosaic.
The work is signed Dioscurides of Samos, but it is not clear whether he was the author of the mosaic or of the painting from which it was copied. The scene shows a sorceress (on the right) and her clients. All the women are wearing comic masks and have tightly clenched hands.
From Pompeii, Villa of Cicero.
Naples, National Archaeological Museum

depicting the defeat of the Persian king Darius by Alexander the Great (p. 72–73), is a copy of a famous 4th-century Greek painting. It is made up of thousands of small marble cubes or *tesserae* in varying tones of brown, gray, yellow and red. The technique of mosaic work consisted of laying onto a foundation of cement composed of various layers of lime mixed with pebbles and plaster the cubical fragments of marble or vitreous paste of different colors which make up the design. The mosaicist followed the lines of a drawing traced on the last layer of plaster and demonstrated his skill in developing form and color, and rendering contrasts of shade and light. In general mosaics were executed on the spot although the central figure or subject, which required more accurate workmanship and more refined materials, was apt to be prepared on a specially designed panel—the *emblema*—in the artisan's workshop and then inserted into the finished pavement.

According to his means the client chose the subject from the decorative or figurative subjects that the artist could offer; and more often than not a copy of a particularly famous painting was requested because in that epoch there was as much demand for a good copy as for an original.

The subjects, the colors, the forms and the composition of the mosaics—whether figurative or abstractly decorative—are of the utmost importance for us because, going far beyond a question of purely individual aesthetic enjoyment, they are the most valid documents still available illustrating Greek painting. Frescoes and easel paintings using tempera on wood have all been lost even if we know from

74

Right
PORTRAIT OF A LADY
Mosaic emblema, 10″ × 8″.
Found in the cubiculum of a house, this unique floor mosaic portrays a young woman of a rich family—probably the *domina* of the house, as indicated by the jewelry and the dress.
From Pompeii.
Naples, National Archaeological Museum.

P. 76
CAT DEVOURING A PARTRIDGE and DUCKS WITH BIRDS AND FISH
Mosaic emblema.
Dating from the 1st century B.O., this mosaic was set originally in the floor of a room in the House of the Faun. These two different scenes display a keen observation of animal life.
From Pompeii, House of the Faun.
Naples, National Archaeological Museum

P. 77
CREATURES OF THE SEA
Mosaic emblema.
The tesserae of this mosaic—one of several representing marine life—are very small and allow the graphic vividness of these images. In the center an octopus is fighting a lobster; on the left a small bird is looking down from a rock. The mosaic dates from ca. 100 B.C.
From Pompeii.
Naples, National Archaeological Museum.

Above
A bronze WIND INSTRUMENT which was probably played during religious ceremonies.

Upper left
HEATING APPARATUS
Bronze.
Stoves of this design were part of kitchen equipment. The liquid—wine, water or any other—was poured into the cylindrical container at left, from which it passed into the hollow walls of the round firebox. The hot liquid was drawn off through the tap on the right.
From Stabiae.
Naples, National Archaeological Museum.

Left
A group of GLASS OBJECTS and gold beads found in Pompeii. The bird at the further edge is a perfume bottle. Containers of the latter kind were sealed at the factory and opened by breaking the tip of the tail.

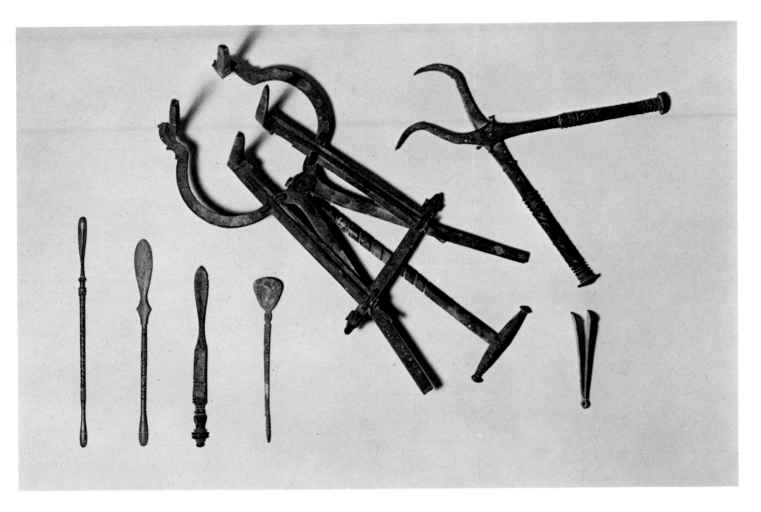

SURGICAL INSTRUMENTS
Bronze and iron.
Found in one of the most ancient houses in
Pompeii, these instruments testify to the
advanced state of medicine in the 1st century
A.D. In the center is a speculum, on the right,
forceps.
From Pompeii, House of the Surgeon.
Naples, National Archaeological Museum

literary sources—the writings of historians, chroniclers and philosophers interested in aesthetics—that they must have been widespread throughout the Hellenistic world, at least in the homes of the nobility and the wealthy as well as in the royal palaces. Ancient Greek painting can be reconstructed in its general characteristics from the large numbers of painted vases that have come down to us and, in a more indirect way, from Etruscan tomb paintings—which seem to be alien to the traditions of that people. What seems to be the culminating moment of Greek pictorial culture—the Hellenistic age from the 3rd century B.C. to the 1st century A.D.—is documented, instead, by the mosaics discovered in southern Italy as well as in the cities of Asia Minor and northern Africa. It is thanks to these that we can presume that the refined and cosmopolitan civilization of the Hellenistic world understood perfectly the art of realistically portraying man in a natural environment, as distinguished from particular forms of idealization. In other words, it can be said that an elegant, but precise, depiction of the physical world in all its aspects was appreciated, in accordance with an aesthetic conception that can be traced back to Aristotle.

The mosaics of Pompeii which can be dated from the 2nd century B.C. to the extinction of the city offer us a vast, even if not complete, panorama of Hellenistic taste. The great "historical painting" of the *Battle of Issus* in the House of the Faun is without question the most important because, from a strictly stylistic point of view, it reveals an extremely complex figurative language that in its expressive achievements is comparable to that of a Piero della Francesca or a Velasquez in Western painting. It is, furthermore, the only mosaic that documents what must have been the official painting of the numerous courts of the Hellenistic world: a type that is analogous, perhaps, to the epic saga of the best of Napoleonic painting.

The technique of mosaic, however, was also commonly resorted to for many other types of representation, such as portraits (p. 75), shop signs with scenes illustrating the particular items traded, symbolic representations or *emblema* of life and death (p. 54), still-lifes and animal subjects (p. 76), and theatrical scenes (p. 36–37, 74). Themes inherited from Alexandria and particularly loved in Pompeii were the so-called Nilotic scenes and, above all, the famous fishpools. With the same precision and passion for nature that characterized the animal scenes, the "fishpools" portrayed marine life with its aquatic plants and inhabitants, including all types of shellfish, arranged with elegant and natural asymmetry around a large centrally placed octopus (p. 77).

PLASTER CASTS OF VICTIMS of the eruption who died by suffocation. The casts were obtained by filling with liquid plaster the hollow shapes left by the hardening of the lava around the corpses. This method of reproducing the shapes of bodies, wooden objects, foodstuffs, was discovered by Giuseppe Fiorelli in 1864.

MYTHOLOGICAL SCENE
Mural painting.
This panel, with shutters painted in
trompe-l'oeil, belongs to a group decorating
the gallery of the House of the Cryptoporticus.
It depicts Alcestis' farewell to her husband; on
the right, Charon is waiting in his boat.
Pompeii, House of the Cryptoporticus.

PORTRAITURE.

Very few portraits whether painted, sculpted or in mosaic, have been found in
Pompeii. This particular type of artistic production, however, reveals certain
characteristics that are directly linked to exclusively Roman domestic customs.
The sort of portrait that developed in Rome toward the middle of the second
century B.C. and then spread to the provinces had a unique origin. The great
patriarchal families of Rome had been granted the privilege of the *ius imaginum:*
the right and custom to display images of their ancestors on a domestic altar set
up in the atrium of their homes. When a member of a family died, a wax effigy of
the deceased was prepared immediately and the effigy was carried in the funeral
procession, the ceremony terminating with orations praising the civic virtues and
military valor of the departed. By this ceremony a family asserted in practice the
prestige and importance of its lineage, and the small altar with the ancestral
portraits—the *lararium*—became a symbol of nobility (p. 111).

From literary sources we know that during the 2nd century B.C. the wax effigies
were replaced by marble or bronze busts or portraits on wooden panels; these
were often copied because, when a noblewoman married into another family or
members of a family set up their own homes, they all maintained the right to
have a *lararium* with portraits of all their ancestors. At the time of Augustus,

PORTRAIT OF A YOUNG WOMAN
Mural painting; diameter 11⅜".
The meditative and intense expression of the girl holding wax tablets and a stylus shows the artist's interest in depicting the psychology of the sitter. Sometimes called "Sappho," the painting dates from the 1st century A.D.
From Pompeii.
Naples, National Archaeological Museum

moreover, the *ius imaginum* was extended to the sons of those who had occupied important public offices or had succeeded, thanks to wealth, in achieving membership in the senate.

In Pompeii the few remaining portraits—notably that of a magistrate and his wife found in the house of Paquius Proculus—are, perhaps, only a mediocre reflection of a provincial middle class that imitated the customs of a dominating nobility; but they do document the existence of an old, if not aristocratic family, (p. 83). The so-called *Sappho Tondo* (above), portraying a lady with oriental headdress and holding the implements of her profession as writer, was probably one of a series of idealized portraits of famous personages with which intellectuals of that era liked to adorn their libraries.

The finest family portraits discovered in Pompeii—two in bronze, three in marble—were in the House of the Citharist. This was a large residence of wealthy proprietors situated at the junction of Via dell'Abbondanza and Via Stabiana dating from the 1st century B.C. On the basis of political slogans found in the neighborhood and some interior graffiti, it appears that the house belonged to the Popidii, a family of landowners of servile origins who already in the 3rd century B.C. occupied important positions in the municipal administration, and later, under Nero, had close links with the imperial court. Judging from stylistic characteristics and modes of hairdressing, these portraits can be dated from the 1st century A.D. (p. 85).

PORTRAIT OF A MAGISTRATE AND HIS
WIFE
Mural painting; 22⅞″ × 20½″.
The painting was part of the wall decoration in
the Pompeian house which is supposed to have
belonged to the baker Terentius Proculus, and
his brother, the magistrate Terentius Neo. The
symbols of learning—the scroll, the wax
tablets, and the stylus—would indicate this to
be the portrait of Terentius Neo and his wife.
Naples, National Archaeological Museum

APOLLO CITHARIST
Bronze.
The statue is a copy of a mid-5th-century B.C.
original and dates from the second half of the
1st century B.C. The god is holding a plectrum
in his right hand; his left hand was probably
used to hold a torch or candle.
From Pompeii, House of the Citharist.
Naples, National Archaeological Museum

84

HEAD OF A BOY
Marble.
The boy has been identified as a member of
the Popidii, one of the most powerful and
wealthy families in Pompeii before the Roman
colonization.
From Pompeii, House of the Citharist.
Naples, National Archaeological Museum

Pp. 86–87
A view of the monumental atrium of the
HOUSE OF THE SILVER WEDDING, seen
from the peristyle. The last owner of the house
was L. Albucius Celsus, member of an ancient
Pompeian family.

SCULPTURE.

Some of the finest sculptures in Pompeii were discovered in the same house.
Among these was a series of bronze animals that decorated the pool in the
peristyle, including a group with a boar attacked by two dogs, another with a lion
pursuing a deer, a serpent, and the *Apollo Citharist*—from which the house has
taken its name—depicting the god as the patron of the arts (p. 84). The relative
paucity of larger statues may possibly be explained by losses caused by the
earthquake of 62 A.D. In view of the fact that to date there have been discovered
only one workshop with the tools for casting bronze, and only one of a marble
sculptor, we can justifiably conclude that Pompeii did not have an important
local production but tended, instead, to commission and import statues and
small bronzes for its gardens from other Campanian cities, such as Capua, which
perpetuated the Hellenistic tradition.

The Forum itself and many of its buildings must have been richly ornamented
with statues and honorary monuments erected to memorialize the accomplish-
ments of the various magistracies such as the statue of Holconius Rufus (p. 23).
Further proof of this lies in the numerous bases that have been found *in loco*.
From the era of Augustus, moreover, it was customary in every city of the

Above
VENUS IN HER SEASHELL
Mural painting.
Panel in the Fourth Style, decorating the peristyle of the House of Venus. The theatrical setting derives from Hellenistic models. The goddess, wearing gold jewels, holds a fan in one hand, while the other holds a veil blowing in the wind. At her sides are two Cupids riding dolphins.
Pompeii, House of Venus.

empire to dedicate at public expense a monument in homage to the emperor and his family. It is probable that statues of this type existed in Pompeii not only in the Forum in front of the Temple of Jupiter but also inside the Temple of Fortuna Augusta. The statue of the reigning emperor—together with those of his wife and son—was probably also on display in all the offices of public administration.

EFFIGIES OF THE GODS.
The statues of the gods can be divided into two types: those housed in the temples, made of marble, gold and ivory like their Greek counterparts, but of which only a few fragments survive; and those solely of bronze or marble which were erected between the colonnades of the temples, with small altars in front of them, for individual sacrifices. It can be presumed that these statues, like the majority of those found in Rome, were copies of famous Greek originals

Right
GARDEN SCENE
Mural painting
Detail from a panel next to Venus in her seashell in the peristyle of the House of Venus, in which various species of birds are depicted against a flowery background.
Pompeii, House of Venus.

Left
GARDEN SCENE WITH MARS
Mural painting.
Reflecting the new Roman taste for
"landscape gardening" is this wall painting in
the peristyle of the House of
Venus—excavated in 1952—representing a
garden with birds in which stands a statue of
Mars on a pedestal.
Pompeii, House of Venus.

executed by expert Roman or Athenian workshops, or were elaborate, but mediocre, imitations produced in Campania.

Aside from Apollo, patron of the city in the Greek eia, the most popular divinities worshiped in Pompeii included: Isis, Egyptian goddess of the afterlife; Priapus, an Italic divinity, characterized by an enormous phallus, the protector of nature and commerce, bearer of wealth, and savior from the evil eye; and Venus, patroness of the city once it had become a Roman colony.

Among the early household cults the most important was the veneration of the Lares, tutelary divinities of the home, where it was customary to have a private shrine, the *Lararium,* decorated with paintings (p. 18). But the images of Venus, together with those of Priapus, were the most common in the houses of Pompeii. Yet, as throughout the Hellenistic world, the Goddess of Love as a divinity to be worshiped became the protagonist of idyllic, amorous or erotic scenes depicted in paintings, mosaics, terracottas, small bronzes and marble statuettes. From the myths and legends created by the literature of the epoch there developed representations of the goddess being born from the sea, reclining in a seashell (p. 88), preparing to bathe (p. 91), being furtively spied on by fauns or minor gods, being married to Mars, god of war (pp. 94–95), punishing her little son, Cupid, god of love (p. 97), or posing placidly as the mother of a family.

Right
THE THREE GRACES
Mural painting.
Fourth-Style painting derived from Hellenistic
prototypes. The daughters of Zeus born by
three different mothers, the Graces embodied
beauty, grace, and wisdom.
From Stabiae.
Naples, National Archaeological Museum.

Pp. 94–95
MARRIAGE OF·VENUS AND MARS
Mural painting; 17¾" high.
Dating from about 50 A.D., this painting is part
of the sumptuous decoration of the *tablinum* in
the House of Marcus Lucretius Fronto. The
two deities, on the left, receive their guests in
the nuptial bedroom. In the center, Eros
readies an arrow.
Pompeii, House of Marcus Lucretius Fronto.

Left
THE FALL OF ICARUS, detail
Mural painting.
The rapid, sketchy treatment in this
representation of the legend of Icarus belongs
to the late Fourth Style, in a manner of
painting which has something in common with
the dissolving contours of modern
Impressionism.
From Pompeii, House of Marcus Lucretius
Fronto.
Naples, National Archaeological Museum

Right
CUPID PUNISHED BY VENUS
Mural painting.
A woman is leading the crying boy to
Venus, who will scold him for having misused
his powers. The setting of rocks and trees for
this mythological scene derives from
Hellenistic landscapes.
From Pompeii, House of Punished Love.
Naples, National Archaeological Museum

WALL PAINTING.

Pompeian painting as found in the cities around Vesuvius is the most important document for our knowledge of Roman painting in the period extending from the end of the Republic to the first century of the Empire. Aside from this, the total lack of frescoes outside of Rome, their scarcity in the capital itself and the complete disappearance of panel paintings have all contributed to the difficulty of reconstructing an authentic history of Roman painting. We have only hypotheses and conjectures based on the study of a group of works believed to be typical of the general production and of a very few literary texts regarding the techniques and styles of the epoch. Vitruvius and Pliny the Elder, despite their rather extensive comments on painting, expressed essentially the taste of intellectuals of the first century B.C. with the result that their opinions are only partially confirmed by Pompeian art. By way of comparison, we should have to imagine a man of the thirtieth century who could become acquainted with the art of the Renaissance not through Michelangelo's frescoes on the Sistine ceiling or Leonardo's *Mona Lisa* but only through the decorative mural paintings of an honest artisan in a small middle-class residence of an average provincial Italian city.

The general lines of development of Roman painting, however, can be conjectured as follows. In the beginning a pictorial tradition was born that was

CENTAUR WITH CITHARIST
Mural painting; 11¾″ high.
This vivacious group composed with extreme
elegance on its black background belongs to
the late phase of the Third Style from the
middle of the 1st century A.D. It is one of
several similar groups which decorated the
walls of the "Villa of Cicero," outside the
Herculaneum Gate, on Via dei Sepolcri.
From Pompeii, Villa of Cicero.
Naples, National Archaeological Museum

comparable to that of the other Italic cultures, notably such as found in the painting of Etruscan tombs and ceramics. Then came the influence of Hellenistic culture which must have made itself felt in the 3rd century B.C. as it spread from the eastern Mediterranean. From that time on, mixing with local traditions, a pictorial language evolved which developed into the painting of the early Christian and Byzantine eras.

The earliest examples of Pompeian painting, which can be dated from the beginning of the 2nd century B.C., belong to the Greek-Hellenistic tradition, which was undoubtedly far more preponderant in the Vesuvian city than in Rome, in view of the close commercial and cultural contacts of the Bay of Naples with North Africa and Asia Minor prior to becoming a Roman colony. On the other hand we know for certain that after the Roman conquest of Corinth in 169 B.C., many precious works of art from Greece, including both paintings and statues, were taken as war booty and ended up as decorations in the temples and public buildings of Rome. Furthermore, the more cultivated

BACCHANTE TAMING A CENTAUR
Mural painting; 11¾″ high.
Another example of the series decorating the
walls of the "Villa of Cicero," in which the
Centaur is being tamed by a Bacchante, who is
holding a thyrsus.
From Pompeii, Villa of Cicero.
Naples, National Archaeological Museum

patricians developed a passion for collecting art and did not hesitate to pay astronomical prices for the purchase of Greek originals. As a corollary of these events, Roman art itself between the 1st centuries B.C. and A.D. was profoundly influenced by Greek culture. The evolution of Pompeian painting, however, appears to have been only slightly affected by these developments. Yet, as in the case of the mosaics, it is practically impossible to know to what extent ancient Greek prototypes were faithfully copied and to what extent they were interpreted and elaborated in accordance with local tastes and traditions.

ARTISTS' WORKSHOPS.
To date, workshops by painters have not been found in Pompeii although this might be explained by the perishability of the simple tools they used. On the other hand there is no doubt that those artists worked *in loco,* in the houses of their clients; and, in fact, in many of the houses numerous rooms have been found that were only partly decorated, with work interrupted by the catastrophe. After the earthquake of 62 A.D., when many buildings were damaged, there

99

must have been considerable activity decorating new edifices and restoring the older ones. It is also possible, in view of the unexpected demand for their services, that not only local artisans worked in Pompeii but many others from the surrounding Campanian cities or beyond.

Throughout the Roman world the profession of painting was divided into two groups: the *imaginarii,* or painters of figures and pictures (easel paintings and frescoes); and the *parietarii,* the artisans who did the decorative elements of the frescoes. The workshop was directed by a master who dealt with the clients and executed the most important parts of the paintings, leaving the rest to assistants. Since Roman citizens refused to work in artisan trades, all the painters were either freedmen or slaves; and the latter were even included among the "tools" of the shop and could be sold along with it, often at high prices.

Similarly organized were the workshops of the stuccoers, who had the task of decorating the columns, capitals, ceilings, and mouldings of the architectural structure with geometric or figurative motifs, which were subsequently covered with vivacious colors prior to the arrival of the painters to work on the walls. A specialized activity was that of the painters of mural inscriptions, mostly for electoral programs. These were aided by two assistants: the *dealbator,* who whitewashed the wall as a background for the writings; and the *lanternarius,* who held the lamp and steadied the ladder—such work being evidently undertaken at night. The activities of all other artisans began at dawn and terminated at sundown. Pliny the Elder cites as completely exceptional the case of Fabullus (or Famullus), a famous painter who frescoed Nero's palace in Rome, the Domus Aurea, and worked only a few hours a day.

Fabullus is one of the very few names of painters to have been handed down to us from antiquity. In general, the artists considered themselves to be merely

ENTRANCE OF THE WOODEN HORSE INTO TROY
Mural painting.
One of the scenes from the story of Troy decorating a room in the House of Menander. In the foreground four Trojans are pulling the gigantic horse into the city.
From Pompeii, House of Menander.
Naples, National Archaeological Museum

IPHIGENIA IN TAURIS, detail
Mural painting.
The detail shows Agamemnon's daughter
being led to the sacrifice.
From Pompeii.
Naples, National Archaeological Museum

PROSERPINA RETURNING FROM THE
REALM OF HADES
Mural painting.
Scene from the myth of Proserpina, living half
the year in the Netherworld, and the other
half on the earth with her mother Ceres. Her
return from Hades is associated with the
coming of Spring.
Pompeii, House of the Vettii.

manual workers like any other artisan or laborer and rarely signed their work.
The only signature found in Pompeii refers to a certain Lucius who painted,
probably after 62 A.D., a scene from Ovid in the house of Octavius Quartio
(erroneously called Loreius Triburtinus); also attributed to him on the basis of
style is a painting in the house of Marcus Lucretius Fronto.

THE TECHNIQUE OF WALL PAINTING.

The production of the Pompeian workshops must have been limited to the
figurative and decorative wall paintings, any easel paintings on wood being
probably purchased in Rome or in other large centers. The technique adopted
for ancient wall paintings, inaccurately referred to as frescoes, has been studied
at length but the conclusions have often been contradictory. According to the
most plausible hypothesis a three-inch, seven-layer foundation of various
materials was applied to the walls: the first consisting of mortar with terracotta
chips; then three with lime and sand; then the last three, of plaster made with
marble dust and, often, terracotta dust as well.

To prevent humidity from penetrating the walls, thus ruining the frescoes, it was
customary at times to cover the surface to be frescoed with tiles or lead sheets
prior to applying the foundation layers. When the final layer of plaster was still
damp the outline of the drawing was traced on the surface with cord, lead wire,
small sticks and compasses; then, in order to absorb the color, the work of the
painter began at once. Work proceeded from top to bottom according to the
geometric subdivision of the drawing planned by the artist; the thin fracture that
was created between the dry plaster painted the previous day and the fresh
plaster applied for the new day's work was disguised with decorative elements.
In order to obtain a gleaming painted surface, which was highly esteemed at that

Right
ULYSSES LISTENING TO
THE SIRENS' SONG
Mural painting.
With staccato accents of form, color and
movement is rendered the setting of the
Sirens' cliffs past which Ulysses is sailing. In
the center is the ship with Ulysses tied to the
mast, while on the rocks the Sirens are singing
and making music, one with a lyra, another an
aulos.
From Pompeii.
London, British Museum

102

PERSEUS FREES ANDROMEDA
Mural painting.
A free, poetic interpretation of the theme of
Perseus, with the help of magic weapons,
delivering Cepheus' daughter Andromeda from
the jaws of a sea monster.
From Pompeii.
Naples, National Archaeological Museum

Left
PERSEUS WITH THE HEAD OF MEDUSA
Mural painting.
The triumphant Perseus displays the head of
the Gorgon, whom he killed with the help of
Athena and Hermes. Perseus is wearing the
winged sandals which will help him flee from
Medusa's sisters.
From Pompeii.

time—Vitruvius insisted that it should reflect like a mirror—it was necessary, first of all, to polish the foundation and render it compact by pounding it with mallets; subsequently, when the painting was finished, the surface was polished with marble dust in order to make it as smooth as glass. A final gleam was obtained by applying a wax varnish to all the stuccoes and frescoes.

The colors were derived from various minerals reduced to fine powder and made into a paste by the addition of water; vegetable and animal oils were also employed. Black was obtained from resin, resinous wood or wine dregs burnt in an oven. Sky-blue was supplied by a famous workshop in Pozzuoli, owned by the banker Vestorius, who imported the pigment from the Near East. The most famous, sought-after and expensive color was vermilion (the so-called Pompeian red), which was produced in Rome as a derivative of a particular kind of mercury found only near Ephesus in Asia Minor or in the vicinity of Sisapo in Spain. (It seems that the powder was often illegally adulterated by the addition of red-lead oxide, finely chopped mountain-ash wood or dried goat's blood). It appears further that the encaustic technique, in which the color was mixed with wax then heated and melted prior to application, was employed solely with the vermilion red.

Even if the decoration of a room was considered to be a homogeneous operation which included stuccoes, decorative motifs and panels of figurative paintings, the latter certainly were regarded as the most important. They were generally located in the center of a wall or, if there were more than one, they were well placed at the eye level of the spectator. Some of these panels were executed in the workshops, encased in wooden frames, and only later inserted in the walls; in the majority of cases, moreover, all the decorative elements were completed before the area set aside for a panel was cut out and a new layer of plaster applied.

THEMES OF PAINTING.

Having been derived from Hellenistic models, the subjects chosen for the pictures were largely drawn from the rich literary and mythological patrimony of that culture. The peoples that inherited and developed the traditions of classical Greece had no scruples about freely appropriating the myths and legends surrounding the Greek gods and goddesses, and enriching them with elements from various oriental cults. Religion having been reduced to a series of rites and ceremonies that were more superficially striking than pervaded with authentic faith in the sacred, and the almost mystical community identification with the heroes of epic poems and with the protagonists of classical Greek theater having been lost, the gods and semi-divinities became mere personages in stories which featured adventurous journeys, glorious enterprises of a sportive nature or erotic encounter.

This vast repertory of fantasy provided the themes which the painters were required to illustrate on the walls of dwellings, to serve as reminders of the best loved lyrics and stories. Other sources were undoubtedly codices with figurative scenes—precursors of the illuminated manuscripts of the Middle Ages—which we can presume served as models in Pompeii for episodes from Greek or Hellenistic themes such as those depicted in the House of the Cryptoporticus, (p. 81) and scenes drawn from the *Iliad* or *Odyssey* (pp. 100, 103). As far as the dramatic themes of classical tragedy were concerned, it appears that a clear preference was shown for feminine characters, whether innocent victims like Iphigenia (p. 101), or victims of implacable furies with supernatural powers like Medea (p. 136).

THE BANQUET, a Fourth-Style painting
from the dining room (*triclinium*) of a
Pompeian house, whose owner is portrayed
with his guests, attended by young slaves.
From Pompeii.
Naples, National Archaeological Museum

Pp. 108–109
The small garden (*viridarium*) of the HOUSE
OF THE CEII. On the further wall is a large
Nilotic landscape; and on the wall at right,
wild animal scenes, one of wolves attacking
boars, another of a lion pursuing a bull.
Pompeii.

Left
Alcoves off the peristyle of the HOUSE OF MENANDER. The painting in the foreground is regarded as a portrait of the 4th-century B.C. Greek poet-dramatist Menander. The adjoining alcove with stuccoed vault is decorated with a garden scene.

The LARARIUM OF THE HOUSE OF MENANDER, in a niche off the peristyle, consisting of a little altar with portrait busts of ancestors.

GOLD BULLA from the House of Menander. This jewel is of the type worn on a necklace by Roman children of free birth. Naples, National Archaeological Museum

A tone of pathos characterizes the depictions of events in the lives of unhappy personages such as Hero and Leander, the couple who died for love's sake, or Icarus, who was widely portrayed in Pompeii in his audacious attempt to fly in defiance of a pitiless fate (p. 96). The episodes drawn from the myths of the gods were deliberately sentimental, especially those in which females were protagonists, as in the rape of Europa by Jupiter disguised as a bull, and Omphale holding a weak and defenseless Hercules in her power. The two most beloved heroes seem to have been Theseus, slayer of the Minotaur, who was always portrayed with the monster at his feet, with children and girls thanking him for their liberation; and, secondly, Perseus, who killed the Medusa of the serpent-like hair (p. 104), and freed Andromeda from the sea monster (p. 105).

BACCHUS AND HIS TRAIN.
A city that had the wine trade as one of its most important sources of wealth could be expected to have numerous effigies of Bacchus, god of the vineyards. The god is represented in the festive scenes of his triumph with his train of

satyrs, musicians and bacchanals extolling the new wine (pp. 112, 129, 131, 140, 141, 143), or with Ariadne, whom he found in Naxos where she had been abandoned by Theseus. A typically Pompeian portrayal seems to be that of Bacchus draped in fruit with Vesuvius covered with grapes in the background, as a propitiatory symbol of the fruitfulness of the earth (p. 18).

The personages of the Bacchic procession were also quite often introduced in small scenes of a highly erotic or amorous type, in the decorative friezes that subdivided the walls, and in architectonic elements of a fantastic character (p. 125). These Bacchic figures were often joined by winged youths, cupids, or nudes resembling Eros in the processions of which they were a part, along with their female companions, the *psychai* (p. 124).

In addition to the myths, the repertory of Pompeian painting occasionally included scenes of daily life such as the famous *Bakery Shop* (p. 56) and imitations of theatrical scenery (pp. 138, 158). There were also still-lifes, with fruit, fish or game, or objects of daily use such as plates, glasses and writing instruments. The depiction of gardens with plants and birds reflected Hellenistic taste in its love of nature (pp. 89, 92, 139). Semifantastic variations on these themes are the Nilotic scenes with plants, animals and fluvial divinities, or the amusing episodes of pygmies contending with tigers and hippopotami depicted in a lively expressionistic style.

HOUSE OF MENANDER.
The House of Menander, one of the oldest and most beautiful in the city, belonged at the time of the eruption to a certain Quintus Poppaeius, a relative of Poppeia, wife of the emperor Nero. Built about 250 B.C., and situated near the

Left
CUP WITH CUPIDS RIDING CENTAURS
Silver.
Two sides of a *kantharus*, or drinking cup, from the treasure consisting of 118 pieces of magnificent silverware found in underground chambers of the House of Menander.
Naples, National Archaeological Museum

Lower left
A PAIR OF ROMAN DRINKING CUPS
Silver.
These two *kantharoi* from the luxurious silver dinner service of the House of Menander, decorated with olive branches in deep relief, date from the Augustan age.
Naples, National Archaeological Museum

Below and right
A SILVER PLATE for fruit or cakes in the shape of a shell, and a silver dipper with handle decorated with the head of Medusa. From Pompeii, House of Menander.
Naples, National Archaeological Museum

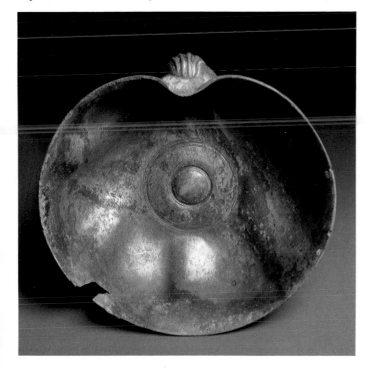

SILVER MIRROR-BACK decorated with the
head of a young woman in relief.
From Pompeii, House of Menander.
Naples, National Archaeological Museum

Right
GOLD JEWELRY found in Pompeii. From
top: bracelet of hollow gold hemispheres;
bracelet in the form of a serpent with ruby;
ring with man's head in profile, engraved on
carnelian.
Naples, National Archaeological Museum

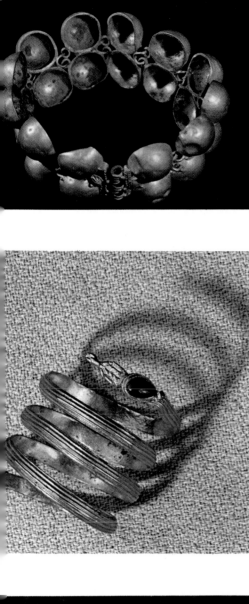

area of the theaters, the house had been enlarged and frequently reconstructed during the three centuries that it had been apparently continuously occupied by the same family. The entrance, atrium and reception rooms are followed by an enormous peristyle with a central pool and garden covered by a pergola, a series of rooms for the owner's family and the largest dining room in Pompeii. The apartment for the servants had at least fifteen rooms. Of particular interest is the private bath made up of three rooms, richly decorated with paintings and mosaics, with facilities for hot and cold baths, and the tepidarium. There was also a latrine. Linked to the kitchen was a garden which supplied vegetables for the entire household. The extraordinary wealth of the proprietors is further confirmed by the presence of an apartment of five rooms near the family quarters that was occupied by a freedman called Eros, who was simultaneously chief of the servants and superintendent of the agricultural activities.

All the rooms used by the family are elegantly decorated with mural paintings, stuccoes and mosaic pavements, the majority of which date from the years following the earthquake of 62 A.D. At the far end of the peristyle is an alcove adorned with theatrical masks and a portrait of the Greek poet-dramatist Menander, whose name has been given to the house (p. 110).

In another alcove of the peristyle was found the *lararium*—altar with effigies of ancestors—for the private offerings of the family, supplementary to the usual *lararium* at the entrance of the house (p. 111). This was the only case in Pompeii in which it was possible to obtain, by pouring liquid chalk into the solidified lava, plaster casts of the remains of the original wax statues. It was on such small private altars that the children of the nobility on the day that they officially became adults, made their offering, their *bulla,* the gold amulet they wore around their necks as a distinctive sign of their social status (p. 111).

SILVER AND JEWELRY TREASURE.
The famous treasure of silver and jewels from the House of Menander was discovered in a large chest placed in a subterranean corridor under the baths. It was probably only a temporary hiding place while the owners were absent or some of the rooms were being redecorated; it was overlooked by the thieves who forced their way into the house after the eruption and died there in one of the living rooms from poisonous fumes. Their bodies came to light during the excavations of 1930–1931 together with the remains of the lantern and pickax they had used to open a path between the walls and the debris.

The treasure, now on display in the Naples Museum, consists of one hundred and eighteen pieces of silver—the most precious metal of antiquity. The range of this extraordinary collection includes two mirrors, pitchers, amphorae, cups, tumblers, goblets, chalices, large and small plates, trays, platters, spoons, bowls, eggcups, saltcellars, cake molds. The various pieces are all sumptuously decorated, the majority being of Greek origin (2nd century B.C.); others, copies of original Greek models from the Augustan age or the years immediately following, such as the kantharoi with olive branches (p. 112). There was also a jewel case containing three pairs of earrings, necklaces, large hairpins, gold bracelets, and rings with emeralds and engraved semiprecious stones (pp. 115, 116, 117).

HOUSE OF THE VETTII.
As compared with the patrician elegance of the House of Menander, the House of the Vettii demonstrates the opulent taste of the wealthy merchant class which from the early years of the Empire began to compete with the ancient aristocracy

P. 116
A series of POMPEIAN EARRINGS, of
which those with spherical segments in gold
and carnelian (center) and those with bunches
of pearls (lower right) are from the House of
Menander.
Naples, National Archaeological Museum

P. 117
A GOLD NECKLACE decorated with
irregular pearls and emeralds.
From a maritime locality near Pompeii.
Naples, National Archaeological Museum

FOURTH-STYLE WALL DECORATION of
the *triclinium* in the House of the Vettii. The
panel painting against red ground shows
*Daedalus presenting his wooden cow to
Pasiphae.*
From Pompeii, House of the Vettii.
Naples, National Archaeological Museum

Right
One of the side rooms (*alae*) in the HOUSE
OF THE VETTII. On the walls are small
rectangular paintings, and medallions with the
heads of Medusa, satyrs, and rams.

Pp. 120–121
The PERISTYLE OF THE HOUSE OF THE
VETTII. In the garden area are several
sculptures, two water basins, and two small
fountains. The walls are decorated with
architectural paintings, figures and still-lifes.

for positions of economic and political power. The Vettius brothers, Conviva
and Restitutus, who acquired the house about the middle of the 1st century B.C.,
belonged to the class of freedmen, who during the last decades of Pompeii were
invested with important public offices. After the earthquake of 62 A.D. they
amply reconstructed their house and commissioned extremely luxurious mural
decorations for all the rooms. After the first excavations (1894) all the paintings
were preserved intact by constructing a roof that protected the colors from direct
sunlight. The peristyle, with all its pools, fountains, herms, and small statues,
was restored; even the flowerbeds were laid out again in accordance with the
original plan (pp. 120–121).

The wall paintings all belong to the Fourth Style, a type of decoration that
developed after the middle of the 1st century B.C. in two distinct types. In one,
the walls above the dado are painted to simulate the curtains and rugs ordinarily
hung over doorways and in garden pavilions. These panels, which serve as
monochrome backgrounds (usually red) for geometric motifs and small central
squares with landscapes and small winged figures, alternate with illusionistic
scenes and architectonic elements (p. 119). In the other type, the walls are
subdivided by extremely slender architectural components interwoven with
leaves, flowers and small mythological figures painted in gold on black, red or
deep blue backgrounds. Long friezes depicting mythological episodes or small
scenes of daily life in brilliant colors are then inserted between the more purely
decorative elements (p. 118).

Top left
CUPIDS AS WINE MERCHANTS, detail
Mural painting.
This detail from the frieze of the *Crafts and
Trades* is part of the extraordinary decoration
of the banqueting hall (*oecus*) in the House of
the Vettii. Other scenes of the frieze include
Cupids as flower sellers, oil merchants,
goldsmiths, bakers, fullers.
Pompeii, House of the Vettii.

Lower left
SACRIFICE TO DIANA, detail
Fourth-Style painting from a frieze in the
House of the Vettii showing figures making
sacrificial offerings at a small altar.
Pompeii, House of the Vettii.

PUTTO WITH GOOSE
Bronze
One of several statuettes found in the peristyle
of the House of the Vettii.

PSYCHAI GATHERING FLOWERS, detail
Mural painting.
Above this detail from the frieze of the *Crafts
and Trades* is fantastic architectonic decoration
in the early Fourth Style.
Pompeii, House of the Vettii.

CHIMERA
Detail of mural decoration.
Pompeii, House of the Vettii

THE FOUR STYLES OF MURAL DECORATION.

Attempts have been made to identify the hand of a few of the artists who painted
human figures and portraits. But for all the purely decorative work covering the
walls of Pompeian houses it has been customary to adopt a subdivision into four
styles which outlines fairly accurately the development of the various types of
mural decoration.

The First Style, the most ancient type of Pompeian decoration that has come
down to us, must have been directly derived from Hellenistic models and was
used between the beginning of the 2nd century B.C. and the Roman conquest in
80 B.C. It was the period when the Pompeian citizens, enriched by their trade
with the Hellenistic-Mediterranean world, imitated some of the latter's comforts
and luxuries in their daily living. The whitewashed walls of the preceding
centuries were replaced by painted walls subdivided into three horizontal zones
in accordance with a scheme that was to remain relatively unaltered in the
subsequent styles. The lower part, or base of the wall (dado), was often painted

APOLLO SLAYING THE PYTHON
Mural painting.
One of the mythological scenes decorating the
large garden room of the House of the Vettii.
Above the panel is a fantastic architectonic
decoration consisting of delicate plant forms,
candelabra, slender herms on black ground.
Pompeii, House of the Vettii.

LARARIUM from a house in Pompeii. In the center of the upper register, the household genius is bringing a libation bowl to an altar, while at the sides are the Lares as youths holding drinking horns. In the lower register, the confronted tutelary serpents face a small altar.
Naples, National Archaeological Museum

yellow and delimited by a purple line. This was surmounted by painted or stuccoed imitations of stone blocks and marble facing in contrasting colors— violet, yellow, red, green. The upper area was gray or white. The whole was intended to imitate the marble facings of the public buildings of that era, an effect which was accentuated by adding mock architectonic elements such as columns, cornices, and consoles modelled in stucco over the walls that had already been painted.

During the years of the Roman Republic (80–27 B.C.), probably due to the influence of the capital, stucco-work was abandoned except for moldings and ceilings. Instead, it was through illusionistic painting alone that the effect of imaginary architectural structures was created in deep perspective and as if viewed from below and diagonally, enlivened with vivid colors such as red, violet, green and yellow. This characterizes the Second Style, in which the architectonic elements were adorned with garlands of fruit, vases of flowers, statues, theatrical masks, birds and human figures. Urban and rural landscapes were also inserted into the backgrounds and for the first time small wooden shutters were used to protect the pictures. To this style can be assigned the decorations of Boscoreale (pp. 148–151) and in large part those of the Villa of Mysteries (pp. 142, 143–147). Panel paintings centered on monochrome walls became the predominant decorative element only with the Third Style, which coincided more or less chronologically with the early years of the Empire (27 B.C.–54 A.D.). The panels were placed in the middle area of the wall, which was usually painted red (the base or dado generally being black, and the upper part white or light in color). Each picture was surrounded by a painted frame

Wall decoration of a living room (*tablinum*),
with delicate ornamental motifs in the Third
Style. The panel painting shows *Bacchus with
Ariadne* on his chariot drawn by bulls.
Silenus, a satyr and two maenads accompany
the procession.
Pompeii, House of Marcus Lucretius Fronto.

Left
The elegant square fluted marble columns of the peristyle of the HOUSE OF JULIA FELIX.

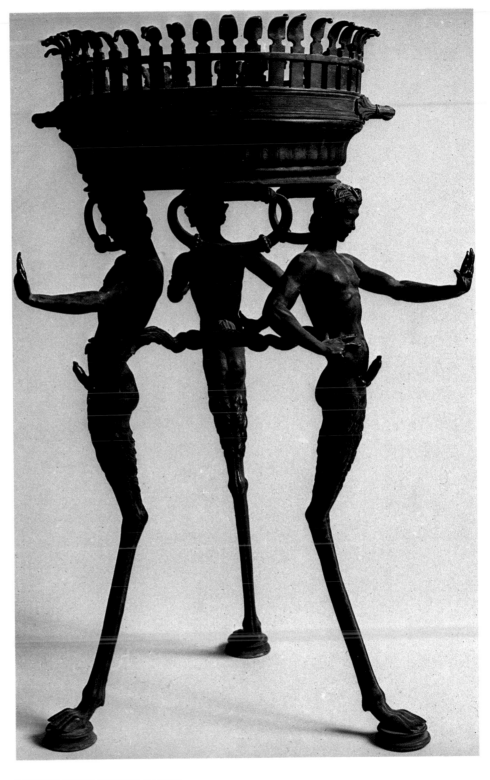

TRIPOD WITH YOUNG FAUNS
Bronze.
Three slender ithyphallic fauns supporting a *lebes,* or basin, in the form of a basket, found in a house in Pompeii. This astonishing tripod was part of domestic furnishing dating from the early period of the Empire.
From Pompeii.
Naples, National Archaeological Museum

Two views of the NYMPHAEUM OF THE HOUSE OF OCTAVIUS QUARTIO (erroneously called Loreius Tiburtinus). The garden is crossed by a canal (*euripus*) which could overflow, symbolizing the annual flooding of the Nile.

decorated with architectonic motifs; and the entire wall was further subdivided by candelabra and very slender and elegant garlands and floral sprays (p. 127).

FLOOR MOSAICS.

Along with the varied styles in the decoration of the walls, the floors for the rooms were modified so as to harmonize with the forms and colors of the wall paintings. The prevalent method of paving in Pompeii was the so-called "*cocciopesto*," a reddish mixture of lime and potsherds of terracotta tiles and amphorae. Along the borders of the room white, black or colored stones were usually inserted into the cement to form simple geometric designs. This type of mosaic became popular in the years of the Republic, and in the sumptuous Second Style was enriched by a large variety of polychrome or black and white geometric motifs, ranging from networks of cubes and rhombi seen in perspective to windings and interlacings, checkerboards of squares and triangles, linked circles, wavy or figure-eight motifs, rosettes and stars.

Whereas the black and white mosaics with curvilinear motifs continued throughout the period of the Third Style, great figured compositions came to dominate in the following era. Small figural representations that could be inserted in the center of the pavement—the *emblemata*—had already appeared in the years preceding the Roman conquest when the walls were still completely devoid of figures, but these were destined to disappear in favor of geometric designs. Finally, in the last period of Pompeii, compositions with mythological

130

DANCING MAENAD
Mural painting.
Detail of a Third-Style frieze decoration of a
room in the House of the Four Styles.

episodes, Nilotic or African scenes, animals, plants, fish or birds virtually invaded the pavements, especially in the most luxurious private baths. In addition to mosaic, which was often enlivened by the use of colored glass—blue, green, red, white, and even gold (ie. gold leaf applied under the glass surface)—marble intarsia was also employed.

THE POMPEIAN GARDEN.

The art of gardening, which had a particular attraction for the aristocrats and intellectuals of the epoch, was among the cultural fashions imported from the Hellenistic cities during the early years of the Empire. The garden was looked upon as a sacred place that stimulated meditation on the mysteries of nature and encouraged offerings to its patron divinities such as Venus—goddess of fertility and the rebirth of spring—and Dionysus-Bacchus, celebrated in Greece with esoteric rites. This mystical conception, however, did not prevent the Roman and likewise the Pompeian garden from becoming in practice an ideal place for receiving friends, holding banquets, making love.

Originally almost all the Pompeian houses of the well-to-do citizens had an enclosure for the cultivation of fruit and vegetables for family consumption. Beginning with the age of Augustus many of these were transformed into formal gardens because only the residents in the less densely settled area around the Amphitheater could afford the luxury of kitchen gardens of vast dimensions. The alternative was to embellish the larger peristyles with small trees and

131

Top left
BASIN FOR SACRED LIBATIONS
Bronze; height 4¾", diam. 15⅜".
Basins of this type were used in antiquity for ritual ablutions, or given as trophies to the winners of athletic contests.
From Pompeii.
Naples, National Archaeological Museum

Lower left
RED POTTERY BOWL
Made of the so-called *sigillata* terracotta, with stamped decoration.
From Pompeii.
Naples, National Archaeological Museum

THREE PITCHERS AND A CHALICE
Blue glass of Pozzuoli.
These objects were very often modeled on
similar versions in silver or bronze.
From a house in Pompeii.
Naples, National Archaeological Museum

shrubbery, as can be seen in the House of the Vettii (pp. 120–121) and the House of the Golden Cupids.

Careful study of the paintings of the period reveals that flowers were extremely rare, generally restricted to wild roses and violets; whereas clumps of evergreen shrubbery, aromatic plants such as sage, myrtle, rosemary and laurel, as well as such fruit trees as the olive, the lemon and the cherry—the latter imported by Lucullus from the Near East about 70 B.C.—were all common. Grape vines were cultivated not only for the fruit and the wine but also for the shady arbors they provided. In other words, the choice was oriented toward those plants that grow naturally in the area and could subsist without suffering during long periods of drought.

WATER AND FOUNTAINS.
The gardens were often embellished with a series of additions that were inspired by the sacro-idyllic conception of nature and that made these centers of home life all the more delightful. Water was considered to be the fount of life and for its conservation marble-lined pools were sunk into the terrain; these were further ornamented with columns and fountains of various types surmounted by bronze or marble statues from which the water spouted. There was also a particular sort of long and narrow canal—the *euripus*—crossed by miniature marble bridges and interspersed with tiny waterfalls fancifully representing the

133

NYMPHAEUM
The mosaic and shell-decorated fountain in the garden of the House of the Great Fountain. In the center of the curved recess at the back of the fountain, the head of Oceanus in mosaic is immediately above the water outlet. In front of the niche at either side are marble tragic masks; and in the fountain itself is a bronze statuette of a boy with a dolphin (which is now a cast of the original).
Pompeii, House of the Great Fountain.

course of the Nile, while at the same time serving as a necessary means of irrigation (p. 130). The grotto—the *nymphaeum*—was a kind of small domed temple faced with mosaic and containing a little shell-shaped pool with a network of jets of water. Another appendage of a garden was the summer dining room—the *triclinium*—which was formed solely by slender trellised columns between which could be hung curtains or rugs.

A typical Pompeian creation seems to have been the fountain in the form of an architectonic niche (pp. 134, 135)—a sort of miniaturized nymphaeum—within which the water fell from one step-shaped ledge to another in a series of tiny cascades. These small constructions were placed at the far end of the garden and were lined with mosaics of irregularly formed tesserae of blue-green vitreous

NYMPHAEUM
Four *cipollino* marble steps formed the
waterfall, and a marble Silenus poured the
water into the rectangular basin of this
fountain, which is considered the oldest mosaic
fountain in Pompeii.
Pompeii, House of the Little Fountain.

Above
THE SORCERESS AND THE TRAVELER
Mural painting; 15″ × 17½″.
Because of widespread magic, occultism, and
superstition in Pompeii, the Roman Senate
promoted actions against sorcerers,
soothsayers and astrologers, who were
considered a menace to the State.
From Pompeii, House of the Dioscuri.
Naples, National Museum of Archaeology.

Left
MEDEA CONTEMPLATING THE DEATH
OF HER CHILDREN
Mural painting, transferred to panel; 4′5″ ×
3′6″.
From Pompeii, House of the Dioscuri.
Naples, National Archaeological Museum

paste that reflected the light onto rows of real shells incrusted around the mosaic. In the same wall one often finds as well small imitations of marine grottoes and niches with statues of Isis or Venus that served for family rituals. Other statues and paintings decorating the garden represented or alluded to deities of fertility or protectors against the evil eye.

Among the finest gardens in Pompeii must certainly be mentioned those of the House of Octavius Quartio (p. 130), which covered an area of more than 21,000 square feet, and of the House of Julia Felix (p. 128), both of which are in the vicinity of the Amphitheater and near the Sarnus Gate. The House of Julia Felix was of such vast proportions that in the economic crisis following the earthquake of 62 A.D. it was divided into two parts, the first one reserved for the owners, and the second broken up into apartments with shops on the ground floor and family dwellings above. A sign found attached to a door offered for rent to "respectable people" even the bath, which consisted of four rooms, for washing with hot and cold water, a waiting room, an open-air swimming pool, and a spacious section of the garden. Nearby, American archaeologists recently (1966–1970) brought to

137

light a large vineyard with sales counters and two summer dining rooms which, like Julia Felix's apartments, probably offered hospitality to foreign visitors to the Amphitheater.

HOUSE OF THE GOLDEN CUPIDS.

The so-called House of the Golden Cupids was named after the gold discs engraved with cupids and protected by transparent glass that decorated the bedroom of the owners, who were probably members of the Poppaeii family, as was also the proprietor of the House of Menander. They had decorated their homes with frescoes and mosaics that reflected the sober and elegant taste of the ancient Roman nobility. The embellishment of the peristyle was particularly opulent: maintained as a garden, it had a large pool surrounded by statuettes of animals, herms and heads of divinities mounted on small columns. Tragic masks were hung between the pillars of the portico, and a shield, oscillating in the wind to ward off the evil eye, was suspended above the passageway leading to the other parts of the house. Along the walls of the portico there were two mirrors of volcanic glass (obsidian) and a series of marble bas-reliefs depicting divinities and theatrical masks.

THE VILLAS OUTSIDE THE WALLS.

From the beginning of the Hellenistic period, on the slopes of Vesuvius and in the countryside surrounding the city, the great landowners of Pompeii built

ATYS AND A NYMPH
Mural painting.
The theme of this scene is the myth of the shepherd Atys who, betraying his beloved, the goddess Cybele, for a nymph, was punished with madness. The setting for the action resembles a theatrical presentation, with the action taking place before a *scenae frons,* with Atys in a doorway looking down at the semi-nude nymph, with a small Eros between them.
Pompeii, House of Pinarius Cerealis.

A garden-inspired wall decoration in a hall of the HOUSE OF THE FLORAL CUBICLES. The upper panel represents the Egyptian god Apis, as the sacred bull of Memphis; in the panel below, the god Bacchus discovers a reclining nymph.

HERM WITH THE HEAD OF FAUNUS
Polychrome marble and bronze; 3′ 4½″ h.
One of the oldest and most popular of Roman
deities, Faunus was the tutelary spirit of fields
and flocks. This type of rectangular pillar,
commonly endowed with male attributes and
surmounted by a human head—by which
Faunus is here represented—was originally
dedicated to the god Hermes (likewise sacred
to pastoral fertility), and was thus called a
herm. Herms were frequently placed in
gardens and at crossroads as protection against
evil spirits.
From Pompeii.
Naples, National Archaeological Museum

A PUTTO POURING WATER
Marble.
Statuette from the garden area in the peristyle of the House of the Vettii. The boy is pouring water from a goatskin.
Pompeii, House of the Vettii.

numerous villas. In accordance with a custom that was to be perpetuated in later times with the Venetian villas of Palladio, the aristocratic country houses of England, and the southern plantation homes of the United States, the Pompeian villas served both as residences for the owners' families and as centers of agricultural activities. The proprietors visited them for vacations during the summer and, simultaneously, for overseeing the harvesting of the crops.

The architecture of these villas reflects the dual function they were designed to carry out: they were much larger than the usual urban dwellings; with their numerous rooms they could supply lodging for an enormous number of servants and peasant workers; there were also huge cellars for storing crops and agricultural equipment. Large living rooms for the comfort of the proprietor's family were built on terraces with colonnades and balconies that, following the contours of the sloping terrain, made it possible to enjoy the magnificent views over the sea and toward Vesuvius.

141

Left
The Second-Style decoration of a BEDROOM (*cubiculum*) IN THE VILLA OF THE MYSTERIES creates spatial depth by a composition of architectural elements in illusionistic perspective projecting a deep vista beyond the arch.
Pompeii, Villa of the Mysteries.

Right
YOUNG SATYR DANCING
Wall painting.
Detail from the small room outside the so-called "Room of the Mysteries." The naked figure with mischievous grin, arm akimbo and leg raised in a sort of mock dance, faces a drunken Silenus and a muse or priestess on opposite walls of the room. These paintings serve as a sort of introduction to the "Room of the Mysteries."
Pompeii, Villa of the Mysteries.

VILLA OF THE MYSTERIES.

The Villa of the Mysteries was built in the first half of the 2nd century B.C. but was continuously enlarged and modified in later periods; even at the moment of the eruption of Vesuvius work was under way in the servants' quarters. The owners were probably the Istacidii family of the ancient Pompeian nobility and their land was devoted almost exclusively to the production of wine. The two-story house had an enormous peristyle linked directly with the entrance, off of which opened rooms for the servants on the second floor, storerooms, kitchens, lavatories and a bath. When it was first excavated the pavement of one of the storerooms was found covered with onions. The two most interesting rooms were those in which the wine presses were installed: the grapes, having first been crushed by foot, were subsequently squeezed through woven baskets by means of long levers; the must drained into a tank and from the latter flowed along a canal into a cistern. The living rooms and bedrooms of the owners are located in the rear of the villa, opening directly onto terraces and porticoes that surround the building on three sides.

All the rooms of the family wing are decorated with mosaic pavements and mural paintings; but those which in later years had been turned over to the

Page 144
THE DIONYSIAC MYSTERIES
General view of the "Room of the Mysteries," with the series of wall paintings representing ceremonies connected with the Dionysiac-Bacchic myth. Dionysus, god of fertility, above all of the vine and wine, is depicted in the center of the end wall. His cult was of Greek origin, but in Roman times this became identified with that of Bacchus.

Pp. 144–145
THE DIONYSIAC MYSTERIES, detail
The end panel on the right wall shows a group of four women in a ritual miming the birth of the god. The kneeling woman at left leaning on the knees of a priestess appears to be in the throes of labor, while the nude woman dancing at right is celebrating the triumph. In the background can be seen a maenad with a thyrsus.

servants have also been found to have valuable decorations. In both parts of the house the paintings can be attributed to the Second Style, with its illusionistic architectural forms in vivid colors (p. 142) and to the Third Style with its Dionysiac scenes and Nilotic landscapes. In fact, a large part of the frescoes seem to allude to Dionysus who, honoring the god's contribution to the crop that was the basis of the proprietor's wealth, was specifically glorified in the "Room of the Mysteries"—after which the villa has been named.

THE DIONYSIAC MYSTERIES.

The hall with the paintings depicting the so-called *Mysteries* (above) was far the most prestigious room of the entire villa and probably served for dining and receptions. The walls are completely painted on a *megalographic* scale—from the Greek word for "large writing"—that is, with figures of almost life size. In an uninterrupted sequence (nothwithstanding the fact that it is subdivided into harmonious sections), some occult myth is divulged. Probably executed about 60 B.C., these paintings were undoubtedly derived from Hellenistic prototypes, which must have been widely dispersed (pp. 144–147).

Left
THE DIONYSIAC MYSTERIES, detail
The young Dionysus, standing at the side of
his mother, Semele, is attended by a woman
(Spring?) with a tray of sacred cakes.

The subject of the series has never been completely deciphered. The scenes
depicted are without doubt connected with the myth of Dionysus-Bacchus,
although it seems unlikely, as the original discoverers mistakenly believed, that
they depict the esoteric rites of the ancient Greek Dionysiac cult, which were
performed solely in sacred places where only the initiated could enter.
According to a recent interpretation the frescoes could be a portrayal of a
mimed satire with unmasked actors narrating episodes of the Dionysiac legend.
In this sense the series begins with the education of the young god who stands
next to his mother, Semele, while a pregnant woman (perhaps Spring) brings in
unleavened cakes sacred to Ceres (above). In the succeeding scene we find the
other Seasons and the aged Silenus, companion of Dionysus, playing the lyre
(above center).

Above
THE DIONYSIAC MYSTERIES, detail
The seasons, Summer, Autumn and Winter, in
company with the aged Silenus, companion of
Dionysus, who is playing the lyre.

Above right
THE DIONYSIAC MYSTERIES, detail
A young satyr playing a syrinx watches a
female satyr suckling a goat; at their side, the
terror-stricken woman is the wind nymph
Aula, looking in the direction of Dionysus on
the next wall.

The next scene depicts a pastoral idyl of a young satyr, a follower in Dionysus' train, playing panpipes while watching his companion suckling a goat. The terror-stricken woman in the right foreground is Aura, a wind nymph, who guilelessly had a child by Dionysus (above). The group on the wall at the far-end includes Silenus giving drink to some satyrs, the inebriated Dionysus stretched out in the lap of his wife Ariadne, and the uncovering of an enormous phallus to ward off Nemesis, the goddess of retributive justice, who is portrayed as a winged woman. The series proceeds with a group of women who mime the birth of the god, portrayed in the half-naked kneeling figure in the throes of labor, and an unrestrained dancer who celebrates the triumph (pp. 144–145). Of the two final scenes the first is dedicated to Aphrodite, the goddess of love, who is combing her hair in front of a mirror held by an Eros; the second portrays Hera who remains at a distance seething with jealousy because her husband, Zeus, had fathered Dionysus through a liaison with Semele.

BOSCOREALE VILLAS.

The majority of the approximately forty villas excavated in the countryside around Pompeii are analogous to the Villa of the Mysteries in the sense that their owners resided in them only during the summer to supervise the cultivation of specialized crops. A small number, however, belonged to families who lived in them the year round and dedicated their efforts to raising grain and legumes as well as wine and oil. Some of these country residences, such as the Villa of Diomedes, were discovered in the immediate vicinity of the city; others were brought to light in such localities as Boscotrecase and Boscoreale on the slopes of Vesuvius.

Of the group of villas of Boscoreale, the most ancient can be dated from the 3rd century B.C. and must have been the center of an extremely fertile agricultural area. The wealth of the landowners appears to have been considerable, judging at least from the magnificence of the mural paintings, and from the household furnishings and the silverware. These villas were discovered at the end of the eighteenth century and on more than one occasion were the object of clandestine excavations; fortunately the paintings and art treasures discovered therein, after having passed through the hands of several private collectors, are now on display to the public in some of the most important museums of the world.

In the Villa of Publius Fannius Synistor were found the splendid mural decorations of the Pompeian Second Style (1st century B.C.) with their architectural fantasies—further embellished with theatrical masks, vases and garlands of flowers—that opened onto delicate rural landscapes in an idealistic and illusionistic communion with the countryside surrounding the house (pp. 148–151). In an adjoining room a *megalograph,* stylistically very similar to the frescoes of the *Mysteries,* depicts in all probability a complicated allegory of the history of Alexander the Great and his father, Philip II, in the refined Macedonian court (p. 152).

On the other hand, the so-called Villa at the Pisanella, which has come down to us almost intact in its architectonic structure is of particular interest for the parts set aside for agricultural activities. The family wing consists solely of bedchambers, a dining room, a bath, and three small rooms off the kitchen. Like the Villa of the Mysteries, this house had rooms for the wine presses, one for crushing the olives, a bakery complete with millstones for grinding the grain, as well as the usual series of storerooms. A barn and hayloft served to house and feed the animals needed for farm work. Eighty-four enormous amphorae containing, for the most part, wine (more than twenty-thousand gallons) were found buried almost up to their necks in the lava dust; the others were filled with oil and grain.

The owner's apartment was decorated, however, with fine paintings of the Third and Fourth styles that were recently reassembled in the Paul Getty Museum in Malibu, California. But the most important discovery was the famous treasure hidden in an underground chamber of the villa. It consisted of a complete table service of solid silver: one-hundred and eight pieces which, like the collection in the House of Menander, served all the needs of the owners' table. The various pieces were of Hellenistic and Roman origin, decorated in the same manner as their Menander counterparts. They must have been assembled by numerous

Pp. 148–149, 150–151
A room of the VILLA OF PUBLIUS FANNIUS SINISTOR, a country house at Boscoreale. The walls are completely decorated with architectural fantasies in the Second Style (1st century B.C.). Spatial depth is obtained by juxtapositions of color and accented contours.
The detail of the same room (pp. 150–151) shows perspectives suggesting stage sets or openings into rural landscapes.
From Boscoreale, Villa of Publius Fannius Sinistor.
New York, Metropolitan Museum of Art

generations and were an important component of the family fortune. At one time they were part of the collection of the Rothschild family, who donated one hundred and two items to the Louvre where they are now displayed.

Together with the silverware were found various types of coins amounting to a total value of one-hundred thousand sesterces—a considerable sum when one realizes that the normal domestic savings of a rich Pompeian family varied from one to three thousand sesterces. It has been calculated, however, that such a sum represented only two-thirds of the annual income from the production of wine of a farm the size of the Villa at the Pisanella which yielded other crops as well.

BUILDING MATERIALS.

The Pompeians made use of a wide variety of building materials from the Vesuvian area. In the immediate vicinity, however, the only rock to be found was lava-stone which was technically difficult to use for houses and public buildings. Lava taken from surface deposits is light and porous, while the lava rock from greater depths is too hard and was usable solely for paving streets or for milestones along the highways.

One of the most commonly used materials was the so-called "Sarnus limestone," a type of travertine formed by deposition from the water of the Sarno river that flows near Pompeii; this is particularly strong because although easily quarried it hardens on contact with the air. All the principal structural elements of the public buildings were cut from this stone until at least the 2nd century B.C. The softer stone needed for elements requiring greater accuracy in measurements or to be sculpted, was tufa, used for columns, capitals and all components subject to profiling. The numerous varieties of this stone found in all parts of Campania include the yellow tufa brought from the Phelegraen Fields, and in particular the gray variety from the vicinity of Nuceria not far from Pompeii.

In the years preceding the Roman conquest gray tufa was also employed as a decorative material. Cut into large rectangular slabs, it was used to face the most important public buildings, which created a sober and pleasant contrast to those architectonic elements—the columns, for example—which were covered with white or colored stucco.

During the same period cement began to be utilized; it was a technique that completely revolutionized construction methods throughout the Mediterranean world. Instead of building up the walls with huge blocks of stone set in mortar—a system that was economically wasteful and costly in its consumption of human energy—a mixture of mortar and chips of tufa was adopted.
The cement was poured in a series of layers in metallic or wooden forms that determined the dimensions and position of the masonry; and once the cement had dried the forms were removed. In the beginning the resulting rough wall was faced with slabs of gray tufa, but at a later date the stone chips mixed with the mortar were cut and arranged in such a way as to appear on the surface in regular designs, generally a network of squares or rhombi. The various colors of the stones used, even if mixed indiscriminately, created pleasant chromatic effects.

Since there was a shortage of clay in the area, Pompeii produced only a mediocre type of bricks and roofing tiles, despite the numerous kilns for these products in the city and surrounding countryside. If a client insisted on better quality, a particular sort of triangular, extremely smooth brick made from red volcanic sand was imported from Pozzuoli. Whereas tiles were employed for roofing,

150

Above
GAME BIRD AND FRUIT
Mural painting.
With three other panels of similar subject matter forming a frieze, this still-life decorated the wall of a house in Herculaneum.
Naples, National Archaeological Museum

Above right
PEACHES AND A GLASS JAR
Mural painting.
With a sense of intimate observation, this detail of a wall decoration from a house in Herculaneum belongs to the Fourth Style of painting.
Naples, National Archaeological Museum.

Left
THE TRAGIC ACTOR, detail
Mural painting transferred to panel.
The painting, probably a copy from a Hellenistic prototype, represents a tragic actor after the play. He has taken off his mask and is looking at a woman—an admirer or a muse—composing a dedicatory inscription. In the background, behind the mask, is another actor taking off his costume.
From Herculaneum.
Naples, National Archaeological Museum

Pp. 156–157
TRICLINIUM OF THE HOUSE OF NEPTUNE AND SALACIA
In a small court formed by a *triclinium* (dining room) and an adjoining nymphaeum, the latter is decorated with mosaics representing deer chased by hounds, above which hang theatrical masks. The large mosaic with shell design on the wall of the *triclinium,* at right, portrays Neptune and Salacia, after whom the house has been named.
Herculaneum, House of Neptune and Salacia.

HERCULANEUM.

Herculaneum was situated on one of the last spurs of Vesuvius, which, before the eruption of 79 A.D., formed a small promontory on the sea. Because of its geographic position, Herculaneum seems to have been in pre-Roman times a fortified city controlling the coast-road leading from Naples to Southern Italy. Like Pompeii, Herculaneum was initially inhabited by Oscans, underwent Etruscan domination (600–525 B.C.), then Samnite, and fought against Rome during the war of the Italic League, finally becoming a Roman *municipium* in 89 B.C. In Roman times Herculaneum was a small, self-sufficient center where commerce did not play a great role and sea traffic was modest. Its economy was chiefly based on fishing and agriculture. Because of the natural beauty of the place with its magnificent view of the Bay of Naples and the salubrity of the air—praised by many ancient writers—Herculaneum was often chosen for summer residences and many wealthy Romans built their villas there.

In 79 A.D. Herculaneum was about one-fifth the size of Pompeii. The city, only partially rebuilt after the earthquake of 62 A.D., was divided by three parallel main streets into blocks of elongated rectangular areas. The Forum—less monumental than that of Pompeii—was a sort of widened street, bordered by a portico, and the Baths and other public buildings were of comparatively modest dimensions.

The character of Herculaneum mainly as a summer resort, is confirmed by the existence of a luxurious palaestra at the eastern end of the city, with a great cross-shaped swimming pool, and a theater built in Roman times decorated with facings of polychrome marbles and numerous marble and bronze statues of emperors and officials (now scattered in foreign museums).

In the area near the city walls facing the sea and in the surrounding countryside were splendid patrician dwellings, often built on terraced ground allowing unusual architectural features such as verandas, belvederes, and wide balconies. Precious traces of daily life have survived due to the fact that the city was not destroyed by the eruption, as Pompeii was. Spared the rain of lapilli (thus

Above
SCENE FROM A COMEDY
Mural painting.
In a stock situation of Roman comedy, two
women are listening in repressed attention to
the garrulous talk of a slave. The immobility
of the group at right contrasts sharply with the
vivacity of the man.
From Herculaneum.
Naples, National Archaeological Museum

Left
SCENOGRAPHIC DECORATION
Mural painting.
Detail from an elaborate wall decoration in the
Fourth Style which undoubtedly drew its
inspiration from the theater, and suggests in its
complicated perspectives a 17th-century
Baroque stage design by one of the Bibiena.
From Herculaneum, the Basilica.
Naples, National Archaeological Museum

allowing the population to escape), Herculaneum was submerged a few days
after by a river of mud carrying volcanic ash and slag, resulting from the heavy
rains which frequently occur after an eruption. The hardened mud thus
preserved intact for centuries a wide range of wooden objects, including not only
architectural elements, such as doors, but also many pieces of furniture.
Likewise in this unique phenomenon of survival have been preserved many
paintings fastened to the walls with wooden frames of the kind which in Pompeii
have been lost. In this way also has come down to us a varied documentation on
daily life preserved in the form of the classical *tabulae ceratae,* small wooden
boards covered with wax on which writing was inscribed with a stylus. Papyri of
literary and philosophic works have also been found.

THE FINDING OF TELEPHUS
Mural painting transferred to panel; 67⅜″ ×
47¼″.
The future founder of Pergamum, Telephus,
son of Hercules and the priestess Auge, is
discovered and recognized by his father. The
seated figure personifies Arcadia.
From Herculaneum, the Basilica.
Naples, National Archaeological Museum

THE HISTORY
AND URBAN DEVELOPMENT
OF POMPEII

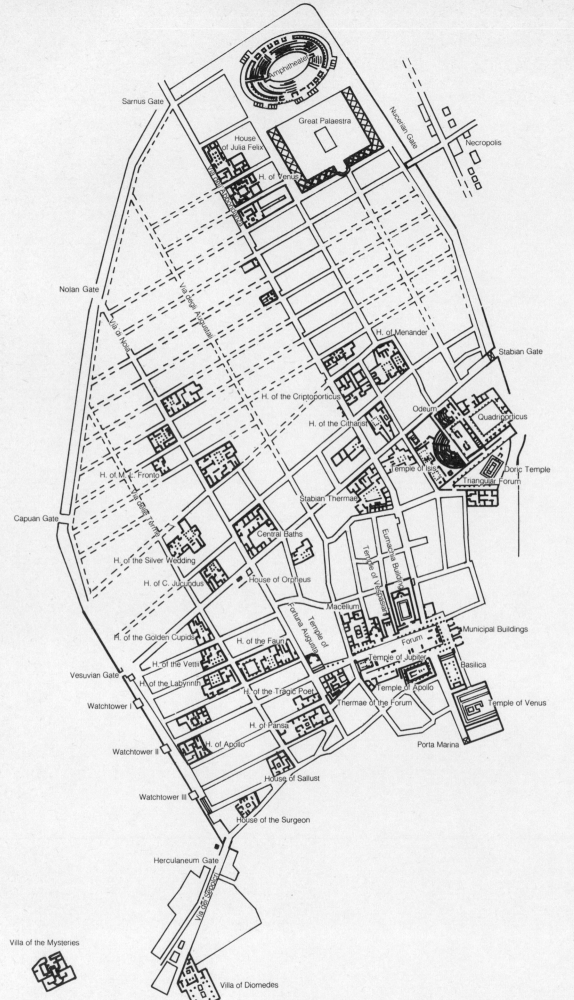

Sarnus Gate

Amphitheater

Great Palaestra

Nucerian Gate

Necropolis

House of Julia Felix

H. of Venus

Nolan Gate

Via dell'Abbondanza

Via degli Augustali

Via di Nola

H. of Menander

Stabian Gate

H. of the Criptoporticus

Odeum

Quadriporticus

H. of the Citharist

Temple of Isis

Doric Temple

H. of M. L. Fronto

Triangular Forum

Via delle Terme

Stabian Thermae

Capuan Gate

Central Baths

Eumachia Building

H. of the Silver Wedding

Temple of Vespasian

H. of C. Jucundus

House of Orpheus

Macellum

Temple of Fortuna Augusta

H. of the Golden Cupids

Municipal Buildings

H. of the Faun

Forum

H. of the Vettii

Temple of Jupiter

Vesuvian Gate

Basilica

H. of the Labyrinth

Temple of Apollo

Watchtower I

H. of the Tragic Poet

Thermae of the Forum

Temple of Venus

H. of Pansa

Watchtower II

H. of Apollo

Porta Marina

House of Sallust

Watchtower III

House of the Surgeon

Herculaneum Gate

Via dei Sepolcri

162

Villa of the Mysteries

Map of Pompeii

Villa of Diomedes

THE HISTORY, TOPOGRAPHY, AND URBAN DEVELOPMENT OF POMPEII

By Antonio de Simone

The City, its Contours and Urban Development

The ancient world could vaunt numerous important cities characterized by long and illustrious lives, magnificent monuments, important events and exceptional men of action and thought who made notable contributions to history and civilization. Pompeii cannot be included among those cities. In its approximately eight centuries of life—which is not long for a city—Pompeii never transcended the narrow limits of provincial dimensions; yet that did not prevent it from having a history which can be told. The hasty abandon of work tools carelessly thrust aside, half-closed doors, necklaces lost in headlong flight, houses securely locked up against thieves all are evidence of what was anticipated to be only a temporary absence and certainty of speedy return in the face of the rude awakening of the "sterminato Vesuvo." But time came to a halt and the disinterred city in a magic and enchanting atmosphere today offers us the vision of an animated population at its sales counters in the shops, of vociferous crowds in the Forum, of agitated howls in the Amphitheater, of the peace and quiet of the flowering peristyles, of subdued chatter in the patrician homes, of noisy excitement in the taverns. Every ruin, every object brought to light reveals a human presence: the haughty portraits of ancestors displayed in the atriums indicate patrician pride in ancient lineage; the wax tablets of business accounts reveal the lucrative activities of bankers; the inscriptions on the walls everywhere reflect the ambitions of politicians, the dreams of young lovers, or the licentious invective of witty spirits. Pompeii quite definitely unveils in numerous forms the fascination of everyday life.

Yet this city is not just the impassioned and vivid reminder of a lost world. The particular conditions of its burial together with improvements in excavation techniques in two centuries of work offer the researcher exceptional possibilities of study. Even within the limits that characterize it Pompeii has a precise roll in a geographic region rich in history and residue of ancient civilization. Such factors not only favored the birth of the city but also conditioned its development.

Between Vesuvius on the north and the Montes Lactarii to the south, the Sarnus plateau—which takes its name from the river that flows through it—overlooks the sea. This rich and fertile plain was already inhabited by an indigenous population toward the end of the ninth century B.C. The site on which Pompeii sprang up was near the mouth of the river where the road leading from the Greek colonies of Cumae and Neapolis on the coast to the north, descending south to Stabiae, Surrentum and the other localities of the Sorrentine peninsula, crossed the highway directed eastward toward Nuceria, Nola and Acerrae. Pompeii owed its birth and swift development solely to that circumstance. The mouth of the "*mitis Sarnus*" was the natural port of all the cities of the hinterland and the crossroads became a junction of extraordinary importance.

To Vesuvius must be attributed not only the death of Pompeii but also, to a certain extent, even its birth. The city, in fact, was built on a ridge, the extreme limits of a spur of lava emitted by the volcano during a violent eruption in a remote era. Subsequent perturbations and lava-flows levelled the surface subsidences and it was on this foundation that Pompeii was erected. Toward the south the lava-flow halted abruptly at the edge of the sea and with its dramatic precipice constituted a formidable defense against eventual attacks; toward the southeast it descended to a lower level, only a few feet above sea level, in the area between the Amphitheater and the Stabian Gate. The highest sector of the city—more than

one-hundred and twenty feet above sea level—is the northwestern part near the Herculaneum Gate. The spur of lava was relatively level and smooth and, therefore, became originally the point of junction of the highways and later (end of the seventh, beginning of the sixth centuries B.C.) the site of a market created with the construction of various buildings by the indigenous population of the Oscans, that became the first nucleus of the city and the site of what was to be the Forum.

Pompeii, buried at the moment of its greatest dimensions and extent, appears from the air as a polygon with irregular sides; the walls, more than ten thousand feet in length, enclose an area of approximately one-hundred and fifty-three acres. The city is crossed from east to west by two wide arteries, the so-called "*decumani*": the Nola highway and the Via dell'Abbondanza or Street of Abundance. Three other large roads, the so-called "*cardines,*" run across Pompeii from the north to south: the highways of Mercury, Stabiae and Nuceria. These various highways, crossing perpendicularly, subdivided the city in a rational and homogeneous fashion into lots, the "*regiones,*" which were again cut up by secondary streets into rectangular "*insulae*" on which the houses were built. The heart of Pompeii lies on the site of the ancient primitive nucleus that was to become the open Forum around which arose those public buildings that characterized politically, religiously and economically the life of an ancient city. The Triangular Forum, together with the large and small theaters, was located on the southern perimeter of the city; in the eastern sector were the Great Palaestra and the enormous Amphitheater surrounded by *insulae* which, although clearly defined by walls, seem to have been totally or partially destitute of any type of building. The necropolises were outside the city walls in the vicinity of the Nuceria, Stabiae, Vesuvian and Herculaneum Gates; and beyond the last-named portal extended the stupendous groups of suburban villas.

The orderly and homogeneous urban plan of the city emphasizes that which at first sight seem to be irregularities and lack of precision: around the Forum the *insulae* with their atypical shapes are inserted with difficulty into an uncertain network of small curved streets. The ancient remains are testimony of events that for nearly eight centuries measured the rhythm of life in the city; and in the history that is thus constructed will be found an understanding of such a richly articulated and, in many ways, characteristic urban plan. The *insulae* that so irregularly surround the Forum are relics of the primitive Pompeii founded by the indigenous population of the Oscans between the end of the seventh and the beginning of the sixth centuries B.C. The Greeks of Cumae exerted a sort of hegemony over the other towns of the Campanian coast during those same centuries; and monuments such as the Temple of Apollo near the Forum are testimony of Greek influence on the primitive Italic formation of the city. Toward the end of the sixth century Greek influence waned to make way for Etruscan cultural forms. The Etruscans, who already dominated the Campanian hinterland, aimed at superseding the Greeks in the control of the Tyrrhenian Sea. In 474 B.C., however, the Etruscans were definitively defeated and Greek culture reasserted itself throughout the entire region; Pompeii, like other cities of Campania, received the urban contours that it manifests to the present day. The city was enlarged according to so-called Hippodamic town-planning principles—from the name of the architect Hippodamus of Miletus, who is believed to have been the inventor and first

163

theorist of the axioms of urban development. The design of ancient cities, particularly the Greek ones, was based on an orthogonal (right-angled) vision produced by ninety-degree street intersections. Such a project was not entirely carried out in Pompeii; in fact, the pre-existing citadel had to be inserted into a new urban plan. The enlargement of the city also anticipated an increase in its population; it is for that reason that we can explain the presence of vacant *insulae* at the time of the Vesuvian eruption in 79 A.D. It must be noted, moreover, that the walls of the city were not merely defensive; they served as precise delimitations of the urban area. This town plan, of such evident Greek origin, was accepted, thanks to its intelligent conception and rational design, even by the other ethnic groups that were to dominate Pompeii: the plan remained unchanged when, toward the end of the fifth century B.C., the city was conquered by the Samnites and entered the Samnite federation of Southern Campania; and no modifications were made, moreover, toward the end of the fourth century when Pompeii entered into the orbit of Roman power.

The Walls, the Streets

The walls of the city, the finest example of the art of fortification in all South Italy, were built of Sarnus limestone and tufa from Nuceria. They were reinforced in various ways on several occasions, although the original contours were never modified. The diverse reconstructions and repairs constitute the most complete history available of the city. The first phase of building was carried out during the fifth century B.C.; the powerful dual protective shield is similar to that of the walls of neighboring cities of Magna Graecia and is clearly indicative of Greek influence. Toward the end of the fifth century the Samnites—warlike inhabitants of the nearby mountains—occupied the city; they largely reconstructed the walls in accordance with authentically Italic concepts and further reinforced them with strong earthworks. It was probably Hannibal's descent into Italy that convinced the Pompeians to strengthen anew their defenses. In the course of the third century, therefore, the external cordon was completed with the construction of an inner wall reinforced with sturdy pillars. A passageway for the patrols of night watchmen was created in the open space between the two bastions. Between the end of the second and the beginning of the first centuries the cities, which had previously entered the Roman power orbit but were tired of bearing the weight of such an unrewarding alliance, rebelled; the Italic population of Pompeii made a last powerful attempt to resist within the city's walls which had been prudently restored on a large scale some years previously and strengthened in their more vulnerable points by twelve quadrangular watchtowers linked to the passageway of the patrols. In 89 B.C. the dictator Sulla wiped out the neighboring city of Stabiae and besieged Pompeii with the aim of subduing the last center of Italic resistance. The courage of the besieged citizens and the solidity of the walls were no match for the Romans; the city was vanquished. Having become a Roman colony in 80 B.C. and inserted into the Roman power system, Pompeii no longer had enemies from whom it had to protect itself. The walls lost their original function and in certain points, such as the area near the Herculaneum Gate with its panoramic position overlooking the sea, the protective bastion was bestraddled by opulent houses. Over the centuries the eight gates in the long walls lost their function as complementary elements of the defense network and became solely monumental portals.

Having passed through the gates the network of the streets presents itself to the human eye in all its magnificence and magnitude with the hallmark of Roman civilization. The paved roadways with their sidewalks and large well-spaced slabs to permit crossing without stepping into refuse or water are clearly indicative of animated traffic, flourishing trade and efficient regularity of city life. It is easy to imagine the sprightly passage of the carts that, climbing the monumental Stabian Road from the port at the mouth of the Sarnus, transported into the city the goods that were destined for trade with the hinterland. We can also sense the silence of the small private streets that at the crossroads is overwhelmed by the vociferous multi-colored crowds of artisans, businessmen and servants who, surging along the main streets, make their way to the Forum to conclude their transactions or to chat in a quiet corner, whereas others descend to the Amphitheater excitedly to enjoy a gladiatorial combat. As early as the Samnite period the Aediles had to take measures to limit and discipline pedestrian and animal-drawn traffic. It was during the first century B.C. that the streets were paved and vehicular traffic was forbidden in the Forum, around the Amphitheater and in private streets, as indicated by stone markers or gates. Simple fountains were installed at the street corners; these consisted of a little basin surmounted by a small pillar decorated with a sculptured relief from which the water spout projected. The poorer dwellings had no internal water supply so the fountains served a public need. In an area of volcanic origin like that of Pompeii the problem of water supplies was particularly serious. In the beginning the need was met with rain water that was collected from the roofs, channeled into the pools of the atria and thence to large tanks excavated under the houses. Subsequently wells were dug that in some places perforated the bed of lava to a depth of more than a hundred feet before reaching water level. Finally, in the Roman era, Pompeii was supplied by the aqueduct built on orders of Augustus. The water was distributed throughout the city by a network of lead pipes that drew its supplies from a main reservoir—the *"Castellum aquae"*—situated near the Vesuvian Gate on the highest point of land in the city.

The Buildings for Public Spectacles

The ridge of lava on which Pompeii is built terminates abruptly in the southwestern sector of the city creating a spur of land with precipitous cliffs. To sailors navigating along the underlying coast or slowly ascending the river Sarnus, as well as to travelers crossing the plain, it must have appeared as the acropolis of the city. It was crowned by the ancient venerable temple consecrated to the cult of Hera and Minerva, with ninety-five Doric columns, dating from the second half of the sixth century B.C. The site was called the Triangular Forum because of the peculiarity of its contours. Between the end of the third and the beginning of the second centuries, when Hellenistic culture was in full flower and the economic conditions of the city were particularly prosperous, the Triangular Forum was surrounded by a series of buildings to which others were added in the Roman era. Thanks to an intelligent and inspired town plan the edifices—which as a whole created in this area a center of public spectacles—were constructed in such a way as to exploit to the maximum the limits that the natural conformation of the place had imposed.

Alongside the impressive entrance of the Triangular Forum will be found the Samnite Palaestra built behind the Great Theater in the late second century. The small rectangular building with elegant Doric colonnades on three sides was constructed, according to the inscription, by the quaestor, Vibius Vinicius, thanks to the munificence of Vibius Adiranus, for the gymnastic exercises of the noble Pompeian youth united in an association. Given its charm and its function the building calls to mind the Greek practice of creating ephebic brotherhoods and the young athlete as the ideal of Greek beauty: it was perhaps not mere fortuitous circumstance that the famous marble copy of the *Doriphorus* of Polycleitus was found in the Palaestra.

The Great Theater was built between 200 and 150 B.C. in the dip of the hill on which the Doric Temple rises. The Theater and the Temple are transcendentally linked in accordance with the Greek tradition which predicated the theater as an adjunct to a sacred place in deference to the belief that the character of a theatrical performance was essentially sacred. The Great Theater reveals in its form definite Greek characteristics: the *càvea*, the tiers of semicircular rows of seats for approximately five thousand spectators, was firmly wedged into the side of the hill and, together with the equivalent of the modern stage, assumed the contours of a horseshoe. The structure in the course of the centuries was restored and modified on various occasions thanks to the generosity of wealthy citizens. Toward the end of the first century B.C.

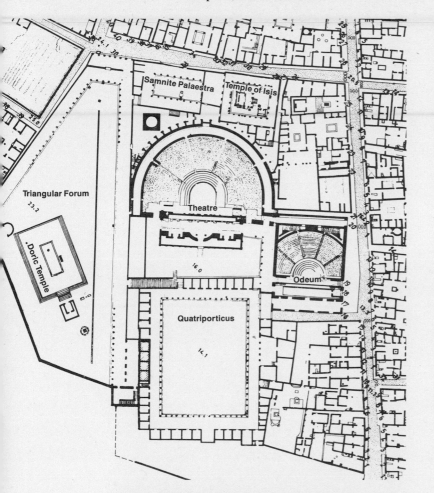

Marcus Holconius Rufus and Marcus Holconius Celer reconstructed the underground passageways, the boxes and the *càvea*. The wealth of the Holconii was based on the production of and trade in wine, and their fame became so widespread that their name was bestowed on a variety of grape. Their political ambitions, moreover, were equal to their riches and celebrity. What could possibly have been a better technique of gaining public favor than that of restoring at one's personal expense such an important and frequented public building? The two brothers progressed in their brilliant careérs and the grateful public erected a statue in their honor in the Theater.

There was a large colonnaded court to the rear of the stage. Vitruvius, the famous Roman architect of the end of the Republican era, believed that a portico for chatting and wandering about during the intermissions was indispensable for any and every theater. The public could enter this so-called *Quadriporticus* not only directly from the Theater and the Triangular Forum but also from the Stabian Road by crossing a corridor at the rear of the Small Theater; in other words, the place was frequented even when there were no performances. After the earthquake of 62 A.D. the court was subjected to conspicuous alterations and its functions were changed: small rooms on two stories were built along the inner walls; the entrance from the Stabian Road was closed and the other one from the Triangular Forum was considerably modified. The court was transformed into barracks for gladiators and new utilization has been proved by numerous discoveries during the excavations: swords, greaves and helmets—some of which were richly decorated in relief with Greek mythological scenes—that were probably used as párade array. The uniforms embroidered in gold, the remains of which were found in two chests in a room on the ground floor, must have served for the same festivities that accompanied the gladiatorial combats.

The construction of the roofed Small Theater between 80 and 75 B.C.—the era of Sulla—completed the urbanistic vision and aims for this interesting part of the city. The Small Theater is one of the most beautiful examples of ancient theatrical architecture: the power of the outer walls, the semicircular form of the *càvea,* the Hellenistically inspired sculptural decorations, and the polychrome marble pavement of the orchestra are all united gracefully and harmoniously. The spectacles put on here were most certainly intended for an educated, refined and discriminating public: the Small Theater, in fact, cannot hold more than fifteen hundred people; it is an "*Odeion*" (Odeum) with a permanent roof, which made it particularly adapted for choral and instrumental concerts. Its construction can be attributed to two magistrates, Marcus Porcius and Caius Quintius Valgus; the second was the better known of the two because he was a devoted adherent of Sulla and had followed the latter in the conquest of Pompeii after having lined his own pockets at the expense of the population of the Irpinia region during the period of the dictatorship. The munificent gestures made by Valgus in Pompeii—he also had the Amphitheater built at his personal expense—was part of a political policy practiced on a vast scale by the Romans: win the sympathy of the conquered by financing public works that were particularly popular with the people.

The alterations of the colonnaded court were an indication of a change in habits, tastes and behavior. Roman conquests stimulated the expansion of international trade, and the merchants, the freed slaves—the "new men"—took the place, as an emerging class, of the old patriciate that had been educated in the refined sensitiveness of the Hellenistic tradition. The art of the theater, which had inspired such noble emotions in its portrayal of great passions, decayed; the crowds of slaves, merchants and artisans that enlivened the streets and the forums preferred the gladiators. In Pompeii the Amphitheater began to take shape. There were precise reasons for building it between the Sarnus and Nucerian Gates on the southeast limits of the city: the area was vacant, extensive and flat; a reduction of expense could be obtained by utilizing in part the ancient walls of the city, devoid of their defensive function, as structural reinforcements and supports; and entrance for spectators from surrounding towns was facilitated. Work on the Amphitheater commenced about 80 B.C. and was concluded several years later: the dimensions of the commitment and, proportionately, the expense with which the city magistrates saddled themselves were enormous. The Amphitheater was elliptical with an arena in the center surrounded by tiers of seats for the spectators that could be reached by either interior corridors or exterior staircases. The topmost tier included enormous stone rings from which were suspended the large canvases that shaded the public from the burning sun. The deeply rooted passion in Campania for gladiatorial games had cultural origins: in a prehistoric era they were part of the funeral rites and religious ceremonies and took place in the forums or near cemeteries. There can be no doubt that they were an important element in the life of the cities; this fact is confirmed by numerous inscriptions painted on the walls of houses announcing gladiatorial combats and acclaiming individual participants as champions of the arena and idols of women. There is nothing exceptional in the fact that one of the few recorded historical incidents in the life of Pompeii was associated with the Amphitheater. In a passage of his *Annales* Tacitus speaks of a "cruel massacre" (59 A.D.) between Pompeians and Nucerians, caused "by futile motives during the gladiatorial games"; the city was severely punished because the Amphitheater was closed for ten years. The event was commemorated in a painting found in the vicinity of the site of the episode: a notable example of popular art that not only narrates the story of the brawl but also depicts the excitement of the crowd and the hawkers who set up improvised stands and began selling their wares.

During the Imperial period the Great Palaestra was built near the Amphitheater; it was the headquarters of the Collegium Juvenum (youth society) organized by Augustus. The quadrangular building was huge—each side measures 460 ft.—with porticoes along three of the walls and a large open-air swimming pool in the center. Numerous sycamores of

165

enormous dimensions planted in the inner court offered shade to the young athletes.

The Forum

The site of the Forum was originally the market of the indigenous inhabitants of the Sarnus plateau and the primitive settlement of Pompeii. It was an area sacred to the most important divinities and it was faithfully preserved in its functions and embellished during the centuries to the point of achieving that aspect of monumental grandeur the remains of which offer stupefying proof to our contemporaries. The vast rectangular square—104 by 466 ft.—was enclosed in the second century B.C. by an austere two-story Doric colonnade constructed in gray Nucerian tufa. The same rock was employed to pave the square. During the Imperial era work was begun on a project of replacing all the tufa with travertine. Statues—only the pedestals remain—in honor of eminent citizens, illustrious personages and members of the imperial family embellished the square which, in its overall harmonious architectonic appearance, must have seemed like an enormous elegant drawing room in which the industrious citizens met. To the rear of the colonnade loomed the various public buildings in which the political, economic and religious activities of the city were carried on.

The south side of the square is bordered by three buildings: the one in the center was, perhaps, the *Tabularium,* housing the archives of the administrative acts of the municipality; the two lateral edifices were the offices of the city magistrates. In the southeast corner will be seen the *Comitium* where the elections for the public offices were held. The walls of this building, having been stripped of their stucco and marble facing, have no longer anything to relate about the passions and conflicts that animated political life; testimony must be looked for, instead, among the electoral inscriptions praising candidates or political programs scrawled on the walls of houses.

Justice was administered and business transacted in the Basilica which opened onto the southwest corner of the Forum; the lawyers discussed cases with their clients while waiting for the judges to be seated, and the merchants made their purchases and sales in the three aisles that subdivided this vast edifice. The Basilica, supported by powerful brick columns faced with stucco, was constructed in the second century B.C. and is believed to be the earliest building of this type.

The commercial aspects of the activities carried on in the Forum are more evident in certain other edifices. In the northwestern sector of the square is the portico known as the *Forum Olitorius* (vegetable market) where dried legumes and cereals were bought and sold; alongside it and pressed against the outer wall of the enclosure of the Temple of Apollo was the *Mensa Ponderaria* (public scales) where two special magistrates checked weights in a cavity hollowed in a limestone slab, in an attempt to discipline commercial ethics.

The *Macellum* (the market) with the money-changers' shops inserted into its facade was in the northeastern sector. The rooms at the far end of the building were dedicated to the imperial cult; the shops under the covered portico sold various types of food; and fish was on sale at the circular stand in the center.

Among Pompeian artisans particular importance must be attributed to the fullers who scoured, cleansed, thickened and dyed woolen cloth. Thanks to the presence of numerous workshops it is possible to document the various phases of this type of activity for which Pompeii was famous. The fullers were organized into a powerful and compact guild and some of its members occupied important political offices. We have proof of their power and solidity in the elegant building erected between 20 and 30 A.D. by the noblewoman Eumachia, priestess of Venus and protectress of the guild. The edifice was utilized as a warehouse and market for woolen cloth and consisted of an open-air court flanked by a stately portico. A niche at the far end contained the statue of *Concordia Augusta* (Augustan Concord) to which the structure was dedicated; a statue of Eumachia was erected in the interior by the members of the wool workers guild as a token of their gratitude.

The religious edifices in the Forum are of exceptional interest. The *Sacellum* of the household gods and the Temple of Vespasian were located along the eastern colonnade of the square. The northern end was enclosed by the important Temple of Jupiter which offered a dramatic sight to the eye, with the impressive rise of Vesuvius looming in the background. Having been begun in the second century B.C. the Temple clearly reveals its Italic origins in its high base and monumental stairs. It was considerably modified after the arrival of Sulla and dedicated according to Roman custom to the Capitoline triad: Jupiter, Juno and Minerva. It was severely damaged in the earthquake of 62 A.D. and was still undergoing restoration at the time of the Vesuvian eruption. The solemn and monumental head of Jupiter found during the excavations together with the impressive architectonic decorations were commensurate with the importance of the city's most sacred temple.

The Temple of Apollo arose on a site that had been considered sacred to the divinity since the sixth century; it adjoined the western colonnade but its entrance was on the Via Marina. The Temple was built on a vast base (*podium*) and within a portico of slender Ionic columns; it contained, naturally, statues of the god and his various attributes. During the centuries in this sacred area the cults of other divinities were associated with that of Apollo. Not only was a statue of Diana the Huntress erected on a pedestal in front of the columns and alongside that of Apollo, still others were added to the group: Venus, Mercury and Hermaphroditus, a strange divinity of antiquity whose cult was widespread in the ancient world particularly in the Hellenistic era.

Deeply engrossed in international trade that inevitably involved cultural and artistic exchanges, Pompeii not only submitted to Greek influence but was unable to reject Egyptian religious thought and beliefs: the Temple of Isis built to the rear of the Great Theater is tangible proof. The remains of the Temple itself, the enclosure for the purification rites, the rooms reserved for the priests and the meeting halls for the

Plan of the Forum

166

initiated are all concentrated within a limited area surrounded by high walls. Instruments of the cult as well as images of other divinities linked to the religion of Isis have all been discovered among the ruins. The paintings with Egyptian scenes and figures that decorated the rooms, the architectonic plan, the abundance of the remains, even if extremely fragmented, create the impression that the temple at Pompeii must have been one of the most complete edifices dedicated to Isis in the Graeco-Roman world.

Behind the Temple of Jupiter are the Forum Baths. The succession of cold, lukewarm and hot baths followed the precepts of ancient medical practice; the baths, accordingly, in general consisted of a *frigidarium,* a *tepidarium* and a *caldarium* to which were usually added porticoes for gymnastic exercises and an open-air swimming pool. The baths, however, were not only a hygienic service; they also permitted the busy citizen to enjoy a relaxing moment and youth to idle away the hours in the company of friends. The ever-increasing use and success of the baths stimulated the construction of new ones and the modernization of the older with the introduction of a more recently developed technique for heating the rooms, the *concameratium:* double walls and pavements that permitted the circulation of hot air in the interstices. In a period of three centuries four public baths were constructed in Pompeii; and the last of the group, the so-called Central Baths, had not been completed when they were buried during the eruption of Vesuvius. The Forum Baths were built around 80 B.C. when the original second-century Stabian Baths had to be reconstructed. The basic plan of the Forum Baths, on a smaller scale, was the same as that of their Stabian counterpart: the plant for heating air and water was situated centrally between the two parts reserved respectively for men and women. The order of succession of the various baths was identical in the two sections but the men's part seems to have been furnished more lavishly: the *tepidarium* was decorated with elegant and refined stuccoes.

The House

The woof and warp of Pompeii's urban fabric were, naturally, the houses. Man reveals his culture and his civilization more rapidly in his housing than in any other type of monument. It is for this reason that Pompeii is such a priceless document. The most ancient type of house, dating from the fourth and third centuries B.C., with its Italic structure, discloses in its severe and definite forms the proud character of the Samnite nobility. A short corridor led to the atrium where the *impluvium* collected the rain water falling from the roof; small bedrooms opened off the atrium; at the far end was the *tablinum,* the heart of the house where the family gathered and the memory of ancestors was commemorated with simple images; to the rear of the *tablinum* there was a small garden which, like the rest of the house, was surrounded by high walls. Almost all the dwellings of this type were enlarged in the second century with the addition of a *triclinium,* a peristyle and other rooms whose names reveal their Hellenistic origin. The so-called Hellenistic house was, therefore, much more spacious and better arranged. The peristyle (the porticoed garden extending beyond the *tablinum*), the *triclinium* and the *oecus* (a room for banquets or receptions) are proof of a very prosperous economy based on the export of agricultural products such as wine and oil which the fertility of the soil and the expert skill of the landowners guaranteed annually in abundance. The Romans had little to add to these houses with their rich frescoes and mosaics, their splendid furnishings and their refined tableware. There was an impoverishment of these residences after the earthquake of 62 A.D. that was clearly indicative of the prevailing crisis. Rooms opening onto the streets were rented out as shops and work was undertaken to add floors: vertical enlargement. Alongside the houses of the wealthy were the middle-class dwellings made up of a few rooms heterogeneously built on no particular plan. Finally, there were the hovels of the poor: a bare room used mostly as a shop, a bed being set up on a simple mezzanine.

When Pompeii became more densely inhabited during the course of the second century, buildings began outside the walls and beyond the areas that had been set aside for the cult of the

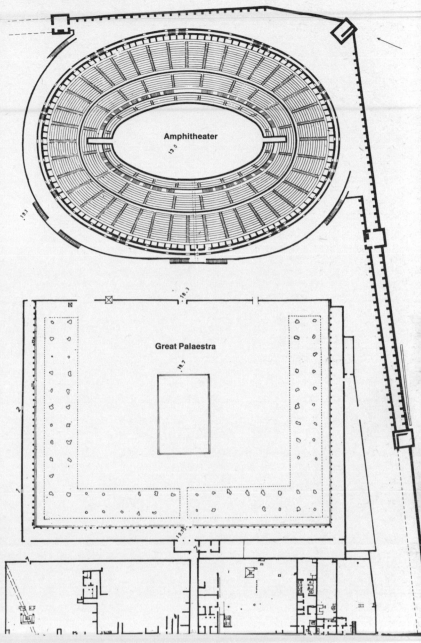

dead and the necropolises. Here will be found the suburban villas built by those wealthy individuals, who, disliking the hubbub of the city, preferred a silent and peaceful existence in the country surrounded by objects and paintings of exceptional artistic taste that were also signs of an aristocratic conception of life that was slowly vanishing.

The so-called Villa of the Mysteries is certainly the most famous of those suburban residences. Having been built in the first half of the second century B.C. it was to experience various vicissitudes during its existence. In the beginning it was decorated with the splendid paintings that were to give it its name; it was later enlarged with the addition of other embellished rooms and was extended with further servants' quarters. In the last years of its life—from 62 to 79 A.D.—it was to suffer complete degradation: a change of proprietors together with a complete lack of interest in its artistic value resulted in its transformation into a large agricultural workshop. It was a sign of changing needs, historical mutations, the end of an epoch that nature, almost as a lesson, preserved in the surviving stones.

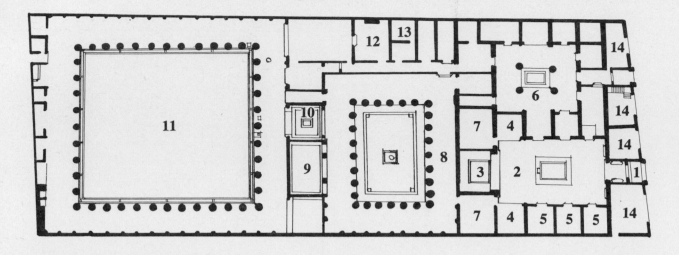

HOUSE OF THE FAUN

1) Entrance; **2)** Atrium tuscaninum; **3)** Tablinum (reception room);
4) Alae; **5)** Cubicula (bedrooms); **6)** Atrium tetrastylum; **7)** Triclinia
(dining rooms); **8)** Peristyle; **9)** Alexander Exedra; **10)** Summer triclinia;
11) Large Peristyle; **12)** Kitchen; **13)** Bath; **14)** Tabernae (shops).

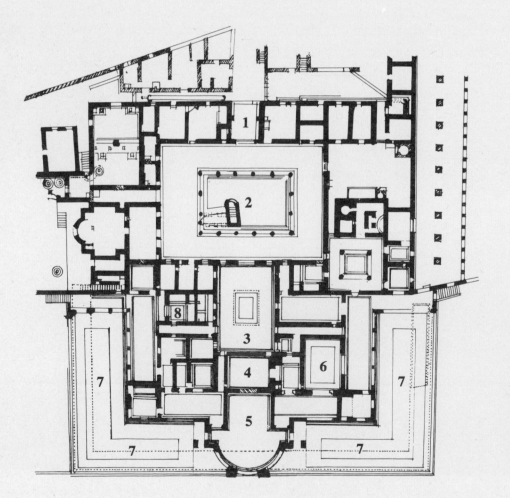

VILLA OF THE MYSTERIES

1) Entrance
2) Peristyle
3) Atrium
4) Tablinum
5) Terrace room with Semicircular exedra
6) Room of the Dionysiac frieze
7) Viridarium garden terrace
8) Cubiculum with Second-Style decoration

SELECTED BIBLIOGRAPHY

G. FIORELLI: *Gli Scavi di Pompei dal 1861 al 1872*. Napoli, 1873.

E. BULWER-LYTTON: *The Last Days of Pompeii*. London, 1834.

J. SOGLIANO: *Gli Scavi di Pompei dal 1873–1900*. Roma, 1904.

MUSEO NAZIONALE DI NAPOLI: *Pitture murali e mosaici nel Museo Nazionale di Napoli*. Roma, 1932.

E. PERNICE: "Pavimente und figürliche Mosaiken," in *Die hellenistische Kunst in Pompei*, VI. Berlin, 1938.

R. BIANCHI-BANDINELLI, "Tradizione ellenistica e gusto romano nella pittura pompeiana," in *La critica d'arte*, 1941.

C. M. DAWSON: *Roman-Campanian Mythological Landscape Painting*. New Haven, 1944.

A. MAIURI: *L'ultima fase edilizia di Pompei*. Roma, 1942.

————. *Pompei ed Ercolano tra case e abitanti*. Padova, 1950.

A. DE FRANCISCIS: *Il ritratto romano a Pompei*. Napoli, 1951.

K. SCHEFOLD: *Pompejanische Malerei, Sinn und Ideengeschichte*. Basel, 1952.

M. M. GABRIEL: *Masters of Campanian Painting*. New York, 1952.

A. MAIURI: *Roman Painting*. Geneva, 1953.

P. W. LEHMANN: *Roman Wall Paintings from Boscoreale in the Metropolitan Museum of Art*. Cambridge, Mass., 1953.

L. RICHARDSON: "Pompeii, The Casa dei Dioscuri and its Paintings," in *Memoirs of the American Academy in Rome*, XXIII, 1955.

K. SCHEFOLD: *Die Wande Pompejis*, Berlin, 1957.

G. O. ONORATO: *Iscrizioni pompeiane: La vita publica*. Firenze, 1957.

A. & B. MAIURI: *Museo Nazionale di Napoli*. Novara, 1957.

R. SIVIERO: *Jewelry and Amber of Italy: A Collection in the National Museum of Naples*. New York, 1959.

M. BRION: *Pompeii and Herculaneum*. New York, 1960.

A. MAIURI: *Pompei, Ercolano, e Stabia, le citta sepolte dal Vesuvio*. Novara, 1961.

M. BIEBER: *The History of the Greek and Roman Theater*. Princeton, 1961.

A. DE FRANCISCIS: *Il Museo Nazionale di Napoli*. Cava dei Tirreni, 1963.

C. L. RAGGHIANTI: *Pittore di Pompei*. Milano, 1963.

R. ETIENNE: *La Vie Quotidienne à Pompei*. Paris, 1966.

A. DE FRANCISCIS: *La pittura pompeiana*. Firenze, 1968.

W. LEPPMANN: *Pompeii in Fact and Fiction*. London, 1968.

H. MENZEL: *Antike Lampen*. Mainz, 1969.

M. GRANT: *Cities of Vesuvius: Pompeii and Herculaneum*. London, 1971.

M. GRANT, A. DE SIMONE, M. T. MERELLA: *Eros a Pompei*. Milano, 1974.

T. KRAUS: *Pompeii and Herculaneum, the Living Cities of the Dead*. New York, 1975.

E. LA ROCCA, M. & A. DE VOS, AND F. COARELLI: *Guida di Pompei*, Milano, 1976.

R. TREVELYAN: *The Shadow of Vesuvius: Pompeii A. D. 79*. London, 1976.

INDEX OF ILLUSTRATIONS

CREDITS

p. 18 Scala; p. 19 Archivio Mondadori; pp. 20–21 Mauro Pucciarelli; p. 21 Archivio Mondadori; p. 22 Scala; p. 23 Scala; p. 24 Mauro Pucciarelli; p. 25 Antonia Mulas; pp. 26–27 Werner Forman; p. 28 Scala; p. 29 Mauro Pucciarelli; pp. 30–31 Federico Arborio Mella; pp. 32–33 Kodansha; p. 34 Antonia Mulsa; p. 35 (top) Fabrizio Parisio; p. 35 (below) Mauro Pucciarelli; pp. 36–37 Fabrizio Parisio; p. 38 Fabrizio Parisio; p. 39 Fabrizio Parisio; p. 40 Kodansha; p. 41 Arte Colore; pp. 42–43 Unedi-Ricciarini; p. 43 Marcella Pedone; p. 44 Mauro Pucciarelli; p. 45 Mario De Biasi; p. 46 Marka Graphic; p. 47 (left) Walter Mori, (right) Mauro Pucciarelli; p. 48 Werner Forman; p. 49 Bevilacqua-Ricciarini; p. 50 Luisa Ricciarini; p. 51 Marcella Pedone; p. 52 Fabrizio Parisio; p. 53 Antonia Mulas; p. 54 Mauro Pucciarelli; p. 55 Antonia Mulas; p. 56 Scala; p. 57 Antonia Mulas; p. 58 Bevilacqua-Ricciarini; p. 59 Antonia Mulas; p. 60 Mauro Pucciarelli; p. 61 (top) Fabrizio Parisio, (below) Scala; p. 62 Josephine Powell; p. 64 Marcella Pedone; p. 65 Marcella Pedone; pp. 66–67 Antonia Mulas; p. 68 Antonia Mulas; p. 69 The Metropolitan Museum of Art, Rogers Fund; p. 70 Scala; p. 71 Mario De Biasi; pp. 72–73 Kodansha; p. 74 Scala; p. 75 Scala; p. 76 Scala; p. 77 Scala; p. 78 (top, left and right) Fabrizio Parisio, (below) Archivio Mondadori; p. 79 Federico Arborio Mella; p. 80 Walter Mori; p. 81 Mauro Pucciarelli; p. 82 Archivio Mondadori; p. 83 Fabrizio Parisio; p. 84 Scala; pp. 85 Struewing Reklamefoto; pp. 86–87 Antonia Mulas; p. 88 Antonia Mulas; p. 89 Antonia Mulas; p. 90 Archivio Mondadori; p. 91 Struewing Reklamefoto; p. 92 Antonia Mulas; p. 93 Scala; pp. 94–95 Fabrizio Parisio; p. 96 Federico Arborio Mella; p. 97 Fabrizio Parisio; p. 98 Fabrizio Parisio; p. 99 Fabrizio Parisio; p. 100 Fabrizio Parisio; p. 101 Mirco Tosa; p. 102 Scala; p. 103 Michael Holroyd; p. 104 Werner Forman; p. 105 Fabrizio Parisio; p. 107 Fabrizio Parisio; pp. 108–109 Werner Forman; p. 110 Antonia Mulas; p. 111 (top) Antonia Mulas, (below) Archivio Mondadori; p. 112 Antonia Mulas; p. 113 Antonia Mulas; p. 114 Antonia Mulas; p. 115 (top) Gaio Bacci, (below) Wipfler; p. 116 Gaio Bacci; p. 117 Gaio Bacci; p. 118 Fabrizio Parisio; p. 119 Antonia Mulas; pp. 120–121 Kodansha; p. 122 Scala; p. 123 Voltolini; p. 124 Archivio Mondadori; p. 125 Mauro Pucciarelli; p. 126 Mauro Pucciarelli; p. 127 Mauro Pucciarelli; p. 128 Antonia Mulas; p. 129 Antonia Mulas; p. 130 Antonia Mulas; p. 131 Mauro Pucciarelli; p. 132 Antonia Mulas; p. 133 Antonia Mulas; p. 134 Mauro Pucciarelli; p. 135 Mauro Pucciarelli; p. 136 Fabrizio Parisio; p. 137 Bevilacqua-Ricciarini; p. 138 Fabrizio Parisio; p. 139 Mauro Pucciarelli; p. 140 Antonia Mulas; p. 141 Walter Mori; p. 142 Antonia Mulas; p. 143 Antonia Mulas; p. 144 Antonia Mulas; p. 145 Antonia Mulas; p. 146 Mauro Pucciarelli; p. 147 Kodansha; pp. 148–149 The Metropolitan Museum of Art; pp. 150–151 The Metropolitan Museum of Art; p. 152 Fabrizio Parisio; p. 154 Scala; p. 155 (left) Fabrizio Parisio, (right) Archivio Mondadori; pp. 156–157 Kodansha; p. 158 Marcella Pedone; p. 159 Fabrizio Parisio; p. 160 Fabrizio Parisio.

We thank professor H. Eschebach for the general plan of Pompeii at page 162. The remaining plans are drawn by Andrea Scognamiglio.

GENERAL INDEX